I0202928

Beauty and Art

BEAUTY and ART

Aldam Heaton

Edited by Paul Dennis Sporer

VALERIUS PRESS

ANZA PUBLISHING, Chester, NY 10918
Valerius Press is an imprint of Anza Publishing
Copyright © 2005 by Anza Publishing

This is a new, unabridged edition of *Beauty and Art* by Aldam
Heaton, originally published by D. Appleton & Co., New York,
in 1897.

Library of Congress Cataloguing-in-Publication Data
Heaton, Aldam.
    Beauty and art / Aldam Heaton ; edited by Paul Dennis Sporer.
        p.   cm.
    Originally published: 1897.
    Includes index.
    ISBN 1–932490–00–0 (softcover : alk. paper)
    1. Decoration and ornament. 2. Aesthetics.
    I. Sporer, Paul D.
    II. Title.
NK1105.H43 2006
701'.17—dc22   2005037948

All rights reserved. No part of this publication may be reproduced,
stored in a retrieval system, or transmitted, in any form or by any
means, electronic, mechanical, photocopying, recording or
otherwise, without the prior permission of the copyright holder.

Visit AnzaPublishing.com for more information on outstanding
authors and titles. Please support our efforts to restore great
literature to a place of prominence in our culture.

∞ This book is printed on acid-free paper.

ISBN 1–932490–00–0

I dedicate this book to my friend Henry Cary Shuttleworth, M.A., Rector of St. Nicholas, Cole Abbey, sometime Minor Canon of St. Paul's, who has the keenest appreciation of Beauty— in Art—in Nature—and in Life. A. H.

Contents

Editor's Preface

If anything can be said about Aldam Heaton, it is that he was driven with a passion to revive in Western society a healthy admiration for great art and high culture. He believed that the cultivation of refined taste, such as in choosing beautiful things for ordinary surroundings, should be of primary importance to the civilised individual. Although he was an influential designer, he took his efforts even further by discussing artistic matters in various public forums. Initially using speeches and articles, Heaton eventually drew his concepts together in a book that dealt directly and at length with artistic questions. This work, *Beauty and Art*, originally published in 1897, was intended to be a trustworthy guide for understanding the interrelationships of colour, form, shape, and texture. He renders his intelligent opinions on a variety of subjects, including prints, patterns, textiles, furniture, photography, and architecture. In this way, by highlighting the elements of decor found in the average person's environment, he hoped to inculcate in his readers an appreciation of aesthetics.

Heaton's eloquence is notable, but what also catches our attention is the forceful manner with which his comments are delivered. He certainly does not come across as a stereotypical "Victorian author", who phrases his words with delicate care, so as not to offend. But why such harshness? As a perspicacious man living at a time of fast-moving change, Heaton was extremely concerned about the alacrity and speed with which mediocrity was accepted, and classic greatness rejected. Consequently, he could not put his faith in the slow, sensitive educational approach to refine the sensibilities of the populace. He became convinced that discussions about art should invariably be allied with strong, but honest, social criticism.

Thus, in his book, Heaton encourages the aspiring connoisseur of taste to embrace the true geniuses in art, but just as readily, he advises him to spurn the overrated incompetents and bunglers. He commends those artists and patrons who understand the principles of art, but also condemns the indolence of the aristocracy in promoting and subsidising great art. Further, he praises those periods in history when art was held in high esteem, but decries his own period's mainstream concepts of culture and the ordinary man's lack of knowledge of art. Finally, as the most expedient solution to society's problems, he wants to shock modern man out of his apathetic acceptance of the vulgar, by throwing most popular pictures and ornamental objects into the "kitchen fire"!

We note that although certain references in the book are somewhat dated, much of what Heaton derogates—the general lack of taste, the overemphasis on the bombastic, the seeking after profit rather than aesthetics—is still here at the beginning of the 21st century. Yet, people living at the turn of the 20th century were in some ways more fortunate than we are today. For example, a very interesting chapter, "High Art for Shallow Purses", reveals the great range of affordable and faithful replicas of beautiful art that once was available to the educated and sophisticated consumer.

Heaton's personal life was strongly interrelated with his work as an artist, specifically as an interior designer based in London. Considered a member of the Neo-Classical Arts and Crafts movement, he was an associate of the William Morris circle. He collaborated with a number of prominent artists, including noted architect Richard Norman Shaw. Besides his work on the ill-fated cruise ship Titanic — he designed its State Rooms — he gained important commissions from around the world.

For example, at Urrbrae House, a bluestone mansion set on a large estate south of Adelaide, Australia, he made many notable contributions. The main entrance to the house contains the original ceiling papers designed by Heaton, as well as ornate woodwork in cedar and blackwood. The symbol of Urrbrae House, a bird that recalls the grace of a heron, is taken from one of the fantasy creatures depicted in these papers. Built in 1891, it served as the home of the Waite family and it was the first private residence in South Australia to have electricity and its own refrigeration plant.

In keeping with his spiritual orientation, he also strove to enhance the interiors of churches. Using an elaborate quatrefoil pattern as a basis, Heaton designed the Rose Window in the church of the Holy Trinity, Bingley, Yorkshire, where he was a churchwarden. Being a traditionalist, he was undoubtedly inspired by the lofty themes and ancient character of the artwork found in the cathedrals of Valencia and Palma, which have their tracery arranged in a similar fashion. He must also have been enamoured of the metaphysical symbolism of the circle and its subdivisions, thus using it to project into his work the profound attributes that he so admired and loved in medieval art.

Somewhat less grand, but nonetheless pleasing, was the artwork he executed for a country house in Wellesley, Massachusetts, in 1884. His original design for wallpaper was placed in the hallway of this house. The print was named "Rossetti" by Heaton, in memory of his friend, Dante Gabriel Rossetti.

Heaton's literary output was modest, but still significant in bringing to public and professional attention key concepts of design. Besides *Beauty and Art*, he edited *Furniture and Decoration in England during the 18th century*, which contains hundreds of photographic reproductions of the works of Chippendale, Sheraton, Richardson, Heppelwhite, etc. Plates of cabinets, tables, mirrors, chairs, chimney-pieces, friezes and carvings are included. The fact that this is one of the earliest English furniture and pattern books, and the fact that not many copies were printed, make it a highly prized volume. Interestingly, Heaton managed to increase public interest in the inventory of his own firm by publishing a book that featured items from it.

Chapter 1
Introduction

Among the prints engraved after the inimitable Hogarth, there is one which represents the inhabitants of the moon; and a rather terrible monstrosity it is. It was intended, no doubt, as a satire to illustrate the horrid catastrophes which may overtake those who propose to be designers on an entirely original basis; that is to say, guided solely by their own untrained imagination. If such a satire was needful in Hogarth's age, there is assuredly twenty-fold the want of it today.

Just when our leading men of science have demonstrated the absolute truth of Evolution, our artists (or would-be artists) are trying to force us to ignore it.

No one who approaches the subject with a becoming humility can question that Evolution is the secret and key-note of Art, no less than of Nature. In the greatest and most difficult of the Arts, where, fortunately for us, the stages of Evolution are most distinctly exhibited, namely, in Architecture, even the boy-student may perceive the steps by which the Greek Temple grew into the Roman Temple, and that into the Byzantine Church, and that into the Gothic Cathedral; all the stages of evolution are here preserved to us in imperishable stone and marble.

The very same development has taken place in every other branch of Art; and it has been reserved for the Nineteenth Century to endeavour to ignore this inevitable process, and show how young men and women can originate things as horrible, because as false (to Nature), as are Hogarth's "Inhabitants of the Moon."

The idiosyncrasies of artists and designers have not unfrequently led them into strange vagaries, but here there is no question of a mere eccentricity. We are confronted by a definite intention to introduce entire novelty, not only ignoring the design of the past, but, as far as may be, in defiance of it.

It is easy to see how designers might have been irritated ten or twenty years ago by the bad examples of every class of design which they saw around them, and our first impression may be that their attitude may have been a mere reaction based on an erroneous supposition that the past had grown so wholly debased that it must be entirely deserted, and fresh beginnings made on fresh lines. However mistaken such an assumption may be, it is clearly within the range of possibility that to certain minds, in certain conditions, such an argument might seem warrantable.

Another suggestion is less tenable, namely, that the strong impetus, which evidently leads many people now, merely to be conspicuous, whether from the mere desire for prominence as in itself an end, or from the commercial idea of attaining to pecuniary access by a new and shorter road, may have led to the deplorable results of the day. Half-a-dozen ending practitioners in such a movement are enough, at the present time, with our quick intercommunication of ideas, to lead scores of beginners to follow them; and just now it seems as though it was "in the air" for all young draughtsmen to try to become designers of ornament on absolutely original grounds. If this book should induce a few of these to accept tradition rather than moonstruck fancy as their guide, it may not have been written in vain.

The essay on "Taste" was written many years ago, but as I have seen no reason for altering my general views upon that subject, it is now printed almost exactly as written.

The essay on "Beauty in Form and Colour" was prepared at the request of the Architectural Institute of London, and was afterwards read to similar Institutes in Liverpool and Leeds some ten years ago.

The "Decoration of the House" essay was written three or four years ago at the request of the Liverpool Architectural Association.

That on "Fabrics" is more recent, and met a request from the Architectural Institute of London; with it is incorporated a paper on the same subject, written for the Architectural Association of London.

The article on "Furniture and Decoration," & c., is the preface to a large illustrated work on "Furniture and Decoration in the Eighteenth Century," written for Messrs. J. & E. Bumpus, by whose kind permission it is included in this volume.

Chapter 2
Taste

❦

"Genius is scarce, but taste is scarcer"

It may safely be affirmed that there is no subject closely affecting our daily lives and habits, about which we are all so ready to confess our ignorance as that form of Art which should be our guide in the choice of dress and furniture and ornaments of all kinds; and yet there is none where a general ignorance produces a failure so disastrous in its consequences. An absolute lack of acquaintance with astronomy or geology, for instance, results only in inability to converse on those subjects, together with a loss of the pleasures to be derived from a study of nature in those directions—no, even a total ignorance of high art may commonly be met by an avoidance of the subject; or if a picture or two *must* be had to decorate the dining-room, a judicious application to Agnew or Dowdswell may completely annihilate the difficulty, and leave the owner safe in the company of knowing dilettanti, and secure of their applause.

But a personal necessity for the exercise of choice, for the most part unassisted, in matters involving form and colour, is laid upon each of us almost hourly, and all through life. A man cannot buy a scarf for himself, or a dress for his wife, a chimney-piece ornament, a pair of curtains, a workbox, a fan, or any little birthday present, not to mention such important matters as building a house or serving on a committee to build a church, without being perforce obliged to exercise such judgment and choice as he possesses.

And when discussion happens to arise upon questions of "good taste," nine people out of every ten instantly volunteer the announcement that they "know nothing at all about that sort of thing" (which is probably quite true), and profess to refer matters to the taste of a so-called "authority." Unfortunately, the same people are equally ready to remark, "Of course, I know what pleases me;" and unless trammelled by the presence of the "authority," who is supposed to have "taste," will instantly proceed to exhibit their confessed ignorance in a practical and concrete form, to the last limit of pitiable, recurring, and irrevocable mishap.

But this readiness to admit a complete ignorance about the laws of "taste," coupled with an apparently complete confidence in pronouncing judgment whenever occasion serves, is not quite so paradoxical as it might at first appear, at least in the mind or intention of the actors. For two serious misapprehensions underlie the situation. No one would object to admit inability to speak Fiji, or play the banjo; he might, indeed, entertain a silent conviction that there is little to learn, and nothing to gain by learning that little. And the same conviction holds good with many respecting that form of Art we are discussing. But this is surely a grave blunder.

Let me take an analogous case. We all know that the ear may be pleasantly tickled and the emotions excited by music, and that considerable enjoyment may be extracted even from an indifferent performance heard for the first time by persons utterly uncultivated in that direction; yet we know not less surely, firstly, that it is possible, even probable, that the ear may be permanently spoilt by listening only to the performance of bad or low-class music; and, secondly, that it is not from the higher efforts of musical genius alone that the highest order of pleasurable sensations are obtained, but that study, and patience, and many repetitions of the same composition are requisite to the listener before the full beauties of fine music can be thoroughly appreciated. And yet the ear may well be supposed to be as quick to convey impressions of beauty in sound, as the eye of form or colour. What right have we to take it for granted that the uncultivated eye and brain can at a glance comprehend the beauty of God's works? I believe they ordinarily do take in an *extremely small* proportion of the impressions to be obtained after careful study; and that the infinite paucity and triviality of the sensations of beauty enjoyed by people who have never given any time or study to nature, are responsible for the general satisfaction in a life which takes only passing glances at the shores and boundaries of things—as children gather flowers from a vague and momentary interest, and drop them listlessly at the next gate—and that the great unfathomable ocean of the beauty of God's creation remains to all such people a sealed book.

And the other mistake is even of greater importance, in its general result, at all events. The very people who in one breath express themselves as ignorant — ignorant of any laws of beauty or standards of excellence—are quite as ready with an opinion when occasion demands, not from mere conceit or inanity, but from a vague and popular supposition that there is no such thing as an abstract standard of beauty, and that the "taste" (meaning really caprice or fancy) of each individual is a sufficient guide for him or her, though not necessarily for anyone else. I don't mean to say that this has been formulated and definitely offered as an axiom for acceptance—far from it. Had anyone attempted to do so, an opposite result must have been obtained. But in a matter where general education is extremely deficient, vagueness steps in and endorses ignorance and private whim, relying on the absence of any canons which might trip up the hasty judgment. And so one hears constantly the phrase, "It is a matter of taste," implying that in all questions which are not matters of absolute and ascertained fact, one opinion is pretty nearly as good as another, and, at all events for the holder of the opinion, quite as good. In which proposition there are clearly some very loose screws indeed.

In order to avoid the rather unpleasant German-Greek phrase

"aesthetics," I will use the common and much-abused word "taste"; but, as it is most frequently used in a loose and slovenly fashion, let me define. To all sons and daughters of man, I imagine there is given by nature some bent or bias of preponderating force,—in exceedingly varying degree no doubt, but something to each; and where this innate bias receives from education, or felicitous circumstances, or both, its utmost development, we have the "genius," or the man of talent, or the ready learner, according to the degree in which the bias has been given, or the vigour of the organism in which it has been placed. If a child has the gift of perception of beauty in form and colour developed up to the point we term "genius," and has the gift well-cultivated, it becomes an artist; if it has the same gift in a lesser degree, and the circumstances of life and education are not uncongenial, we get the man or woman of "taste" or "good taste."

The phrase "bad taste" is misleading, because it seems to allow that taste is a question merely of degree, and that all the degrees are more or less admissible from something short of bad up to something actually good. If we find a mistake in a matter involving the use of decorative art, the word "false" will best express the blunder. The word "taste," therefore, should be used to express a natural aptitude and an acquired facility for seeing what is beautiful in form and colour, and promptly separating it from what is coarse and degrading. "Taste" is the faculty of discriminating, and where no discrimination is made, no taste exists. Of course taste may enter into more matters than decorative art, but it is not now our purpose to follow it further.

Unquestionably there is a large number of people originally possessing this innate sense of beauty in form and colour; but among those born with such a bias, many never have the natural gift cultivated, and it becomes obscured; while a still larger number, through want of personal force and individuality of character, cease to exercise the gift, and drop helplessly into grooves marked out by the chariot-wheels of the great goddess Fashion.

And how wide is the list of subjects upon which people, confessedly ignorant, have daily to exercise their judgment—with a correspondent widely disastrous result, of course!

Let me enumerate: and first, on account of the all but daily necessity for the purchase of some article, and its enormous cost if added up for a lifetime, must be placed Women's dress. *"They ordered the silks and they ordered the flowers, And the bill it kept rolling up gown upon gown."*

And next, not to be ungallant, *Men's dress*—for a man may make a terrible fool of himself by a ridiculous garment, and not know it.

3rd. Trifles for ornament, for presents, and little "nothings" generally, in which, through constant, daily, hourly transactions, the annual expenditure must be enormous, and in which false taste very commonly makes its appearance.

4th. Jewellery for both sexes, and plate,—costing as much as the maintenance of armies.

5th. Ladies' fancy work, daily before our eyes, generally entirely useless and exceedingly costly.

6th. Wall papers and carpets, working havoc in the rooms we have to inhabit for most of our waking hours. Draperies, which form an absolutely necessary item in every room where comfort, not to say luxury, is desired. Furniture for the house, the office, the public building, the school, the place of worship.

7th. Glass, china, and table ornaments generally, for domestic use, always being broken, and so requiring constant renewal. Decorative china, clocks, bronzes, staircase "stained-glass" windows, &c., &c.— generally not decorative. Mirrors and chimney-pieces, involving great displays of real and sham marble, carving and gilding.

8th. Pictures, engravings, and illustrated books and their bindings, forming a cumbrous and useless incubus on the drawing-room and library tables.

9th. Gardening, including the inevitable summer-house.

10th. Church embroidery, decoration, and stained-glass, where false taste is a public horror.

And lastly, above and beyond the range of the subjects we are discussing in their relation to good taste, but unfortunately, as a matter of practice, quite within the range of the ordinary transactions of ordinary mortals, and for the most part quite unguarded by any selection of men for their special fitness, comes No. 11, *choice of architectural design*, including the house, the place of business, the public building, the church, where false taste and blunders are a *national* disaster.

Here is an appalling list of eleven tolerably distinct subjects, upon all of which many of us, and upon many of which all of us, have constantly to exercise our unassisted judgment as well as we can; involving the spending of a large portion of our time, and a still larger proportion of our annual incomes; and to fit us for which not one in a hundred has received any education whatever.

Perhaps some of my readers may reply, "Well, but in nine out of eleven of your subjects a mistake does not necessarily affect anyone but the individuals who are parties to it, and perhaps not even them, for they may never find it out." But, setting aside for the moment the fact that no individual mistake can be anything but a common loss —for is not the nation made up of individuals?—I answer that there are at least three distinct ways in which the exercise of false taste is individually as well as generally harmful:

For, first, the error *perpetuates itself* by encouraging trade in the precise direction of the blunder, and by imprinting itself on the minds of children and others incapable of exercising unbiassed judgment.

2nd. It leaves an heirloom of false rubbish to be dealt with by posterity, which, out of regard for the opinion of the past, is likely to be hampered and blinded in exercising a true judgment.

3rd. It deprives the buyer of a great part of the value of what he purchases. He ought to reap definite gratification ("sweetness and light") from the form, design, colour, or fitness of what he has acquired; but if he has asked for a fish, and knows so little of the nature of fishes that he can be put off with a stone, he is cheated.

Moreover, an inability to exercise "taste" robs us of enjoyment in two directions. It hampers and deadens our enjoyment of God's art (Nature), and it bars the road altogether to the poetic region of man's art—the great world of poetry in architecture, painting, and sculpture. Those to whom beauty of form and colour is a dead letter, only see half the loveliness—perhaps not half—of flower and mountain, opal and sunset. If we are rightly to read the beautiful page of Nature, we must at least have learned our alphabet, and the primer is a patient, careful, and humble study of leaf and flower, bud and berry, pebble and crag, searching for the beauty of the Maker in each. If we would truly comprehend the beauty of the other Creation "Man added to Nature," we must patiently and reverently study the footprints by which Phidias and Durer, Tintoretto and Turner, approached the Temple of Art to add courses to her masonry.

And finally, mistakes under the last head are without doubt *national disasters*. Men, confessing their ignorance, but having no just knowledge of the results of such ignorance, fearlessly approach the most difficult work man has to put his hand to — architecture; advertise for plans, and, to relieve themselves from the intricate work of constant consultations with an architect, "consider" (!) the competing designs with redhot haste, or with a foregone conclusion in favour of a cousin or a neighbour, and vote huge sums of money for the erection of buildings, which in nineteen cases out of twenty never afford a ray of pleasure or satisfaction to any—not even to the builders; which people of quick perceptions instantly pronounce to be altogether inferior to the mediaeval remains among us, and which cannot fail to be an incubus and an eyesore to our posterity, if not indeed to ourselves also. If the same individuals were asked to sit in judgment upon an oratorio or a chemical analysis, they would instantly shrink from the ordeal, feeling their want of exact knowledge; but in these questions where the use of the eyes alone is unhappily supposed to furnish the judge with all the evidence required, people satisfy themselves with the consideration, "I suppose I know what I like when *I see it with my eyes.*" A most miserable blunder! As if the eyes are anything more than reflectors to convey pictures of facts to the brain. The eyes do their duty for the most part truthfully enough, examine the witnesses and report the evidence exactly enough; but if the brain be an uncultivated and indiscriminating judge, unlearned and careless, what will the judgments be?

We have had in times past a living school of decorative art in Europe, if not in England; but unfortunately it is long since dead. With the rashness of boy navigators, we have cut the well-anchored and safe cable of Tradition.

We have not been taught at school even the barest outlines of Art. And as a nation we seem (in comparison with Orientals, for instance), rather deficient than otherwise in artistic instincts and capacities, and have our minds mainly set upon politics, literature, science, railways, and moneymaking; so that we undoubtedly are— the large majority of us—quite as innocent of "taste" as with commendable candour we generally confess ourselves to be.

Again, there is such a fearful multiplicity of things to mislead— things set before us with glamour and false lights—wares recommended by false titles (and sold by false weights). Not to mention the terrible Berlin wool work patterns from Germany, which haunted us in our childhood, and prey upon us still, in slippers, in cushions, in smoking-caps, in antimacassars, in bed-pockets — present with us like evil genii by night and by day, sneaking into the sanctum of our affections by aid of the loving fingers and bright eyes of fair workers —not to mention these, are we not fairly overwhelmed with a torrent of rubbish from France, saleable only because it is novel, admired only because it is "fashionable"—apples of Sodom, brilliant and attractive to the eye, dust and poison to the palate. But French dress, jewellery, furniture, and knicknackeries would not be sold if they found no buyers. There is manifestly a great demand for things designed in the French style, and it is now so widely spread in England, Germany, Austria, America, wherever, in fact, Europeans dwell, and forms so common a standard of imitation, that it may be well before going further to stop and inquire how this pre-eminence has been obtained.

Beautiful as are the Art-remains of ancient France, our own country is quite as rich, and in the later productions of Gothic, probably richer. France certainly has produced tapestries of extraordinary beauty and of the highest artistic value; but she can boast no equivalents to Holbein, Gainsborough, Reynolds, and Turner. That the china of Sevres ever possessed any high artistic merit may well be doubted it might be exquisite in point of workmanship, wonderful in suggestion of costliness, fit "to set before a king", but with its absence of all sense of *fitness* in the sort of design employed, it must, in company with our own Chelsea ware, and the productions of Dresden, be relegated to a very inferior place indeed when compared with fine old Oriental ware, or even with mediaeval Italian. France seems to have been before us in the present day in the successful copying of Oriental china; but we have preceded her in the resuscitation of the art of making stained glass, and in reproducing eighteenth century furniture showing how poetical and picturesque were the houses of our forefathers.

Both nations have had an era of living decorative art, and from both, that era has long since departed. In this respect, therefore, they are equal—equal in disadvantage. In the realms of literature we need not fear comparison; in the complete enjoyment of national freedom, in enterprise, in a growing dislike of war and consequent advance in civilisation, in the dignity of the national councils, there is everything to lead to the conviction that England should be *at least on a level* with her neighbour in the production of anything requiring active brains and nimble fingers.

Nevertheless, French fashions have obtained an enormously preponderating position.

I shall endeavour to show that the French have attained this preeminence by means of an inordinate and extravagant attention to women's dress, with a constant appeal to the sensuous rather than to the intellectual side of human nature; and that it is through two eccentricities of the national character, which cannot be considered as anything else but national weaknesses, that this result has been mainly obtained.

However desirable it was that Gothic art, having become effete and corrupt, should be swept away, there can be no doubt that the Renaissance, when fully developed, swept away also the love of fine design, and substituted the love of fine workmanship. Instead of a delight in quaint, mysterious, and poetical representations of things natural and supernatural, such as undoubtedly belonged to the earlier centuries, it substituted niceties of trivial detail and infinite finessing in trifles; and, above all, it encouraged in courts and nobles an insistent passion for display, resulting in an entire loss of the love of beautiful things *for their beauty*, and giving in return only a desire to display costly things for their cost; transferring, moreover, a large proportion of the decoration formerly bestowed principally upon the house, to the occupants of the house, and so encouraging that pride of life which before long became the bane of society and its ruin. And here, I think, was the birth of "Fashion."

When a court lady wore a splendid robe—embroidered by her own women perhaps,—and delighted in it because of its wealth of imagery and colour, the natural desire would be to take care of it, and even to transmit it to a successor; but when she came to wear a dress whose only charm was its excellence of manufacture or its suggestion of costliness, the growing love of display and pride of life demanded a relay of such dresses, with proportionate *éclat* to arise from their recurring variety. But how was variety to be exhibited? Noble design was no longer sought for their embroideries—scarcely for their brocades; the cut of the dress, its trimmings, its colour, must become a subject of increased study, and a court lady must each month outdo herself. And the goddess Fashion was upreared to receive the plaudits (or curses) of generations unborn.

Consider here the absolute and radical difference between a choice made in accordance with a sense of beauty and one made in accordance with what is said to be fashionable. It is not a question of degree, it is one of kind. If a man once accepts the fashion of the day as his guide, he cannot possibly accept the laws of beauty, of colour and form, also as a guide. "No man can serve two masters," especially, as in the present case, where the two masters may be, and often are, in direct opposition.

Twice at least in historic times, in the life of nations we cannot but study and admire Greece and Rome—a point was reached at which civilisation, wealth, and ease resulted in an intense admiration of the human body, and an overweening care for its gratification—an overwhelming and over-sensuous admiration of it and a pampering of its appetites. It is not to the present purpose to stop and inquire to what extent the human body contains all the elements of beauty of form which an artistic people must study, and study with delight; or how far, mankind being made up of body as well as soul and spirit, the body is entitled to its delights—let much be granted on both heads. It is nevertheless true that coincidently with this inordinate love of the body came a loss of those grander attributes, virtues, heroisms, which had made those great nations what they were. Their excessive love of the body did not make them greater, it made them feebler. As they became more of sensualists they became less of men. But the trade in dress, and ornaments, and luxuries, and costly furniture throve enormously, and in Pompeii reached an abyss of extravagance unknown before or since. But the luxury had destroyed the Art—costliness and sensuality alone remained.

History does repeat itself. In eighteenth and nineteenth century Europe, civilisation, wealth, and ease have again produced among courtiers, among the aristocracy, among the wealthy-idle, an excessive consideration for the human body—evidently the natural result of these circumstances; and those who can the most success fully cater for the gratification of this passion are sure of a trade more or less Pompeian.

Now, the French have two characteristics as a nation, referred to above, which eminently fit them to fill this office: I mean, an infinite possibility of abandon, of giving the rein freely, regardless of consequences, to whatever craving for gratification a fertile imagination may suggest; and, secondly, a strong tendency to dramatise and to exaggerate for the dramatic effect, colour or form, light and shade, action and expression, even to the point of the grotesque; resulting in the production of things startling, things sensational, things *piquant*, things *drôle*. Deeply imbued with the spirit of the Renaissance, and consequently revelling in all that suggests pomp and princely living, in delicacy of workmanship, in finesse of detail, in the extravagant use of the precious metals (or, what appears to serve as well, their imitations), it is inevitable that Fashion should be the goddess at whose shrine they worship. And Fashion, followed with abandon and exaggeration, means constant novelty; for if a dress or a trinket has no other recommendation than that it is fashionable—that it is in the fashionable style—its value ceases when a fresh panderer to the thirst for *éclat* or sensation introduces a new style. Throw it aside and get another, or you will be behind in the race. It means more, how ever, as we shall see. And, constituted as Eve's daughters are, it does not require either a historian or a magician to tell us that a young and idle woman living "in society," and having the means or the credit, will go in for novelty pretty fiercely, and that there will be plenty of tradesmen to do her bidding. The end she proposes to herself is to elicit the admiration of the coterie among whom she lives, and it must be admitted that either sex generally shows itself quite ready for the occasion.

It must freely be granted that the French *modist* (let me use the word in this form for male or female) brings many fitting qualities to the task, at least if present fashions are the best to be desired in dress (though this I by no means grant). The French are clever, ingenious, fertile in invention, dexterous in handiwork, exact in manipulation. And this trade in women's dress is on so important a scale that well-to-do and talented people will engage in it, and can afford to retain the most dexterous and highly skilled artisans in their employ.

Half the resources of Nature are pressed into the service: wool, silk, linen, cotton are not enough; "effects" must be obtained by the use of straw, of feathers, of fur, of shells, of beads, of gold dust—of anything, in short, that can add piquancy to the trimmings which fancy dictates, and which desire for novelty *demands*. But varieties of material, varieties of fabric, varieties of colour—enormous as these latter are in number when we think of them, in light and shade, in contrast and harmony—varieties of this sort are not enough: there must be constant change in the arrangement and rearrangement of the parts, and in invention of new and startling features of detail. Now the dress must fit the figure tightly, now loosely; now the sleeve must be plain, now baggy as the wind; now the skirt must be single, now double or flounced—not from considerations of beauty or fitness, but because one or two leading modists say it is to be so. The head-dress, meantime, of course receives equal attention; and it becomes inevitable that all the accessories of jewellery, trinkets, furniture, and decoration of the house should fall into the same or sympathetic hands—indeed, when once we have converted woman into a hook to hang clothes on, it becomes necessary that the surroundings should be *en suite*. A mediaeval lady was dressed in garments that were attractive whether she walked in turret or bower, because they were beautiful; but if a modern French fashionable beauty is clothed in a silk whose merit is its novelty of colour, it becomes a necessity that the new colour should be repeated in the boudoir, or set off by contrasts in the furniture, till the very walls themselves are covered, not by storied tapestry or fresco, but with quilted silk like the women's dresses! The *modist* has become an upholsterer, the upholsterer a *modist*, and the occupant of the house a dummy to show off their productions.

But even these resources for the creation of *haute nouveauté* are insufficient: more dexterous and telling appeals to the admiration must be addressed to palates satiated with change. Dressing is not enough, there must also be undressing; and here we may see the true character of much of the race after fashion among the class who "set" or follow fashions.

The French, of course, did not invent the *decolletté* dress. It was simply the natural outcome of the first woven dress ever made a single garment with a large hole in the middle to admit the head. But they showed themselves very ready, after their fashion, to exaggerate it, and one has only to look at the prints of the last century to find out how far the exaggeration went. In fact, it is well known that a French actress who visited London lately had thought it best to get rid of the bodice altogether.

This is not a moral essay, and it is quite immaterial to our present purpose to inquire what amount of indulgence ought to be granted to a healthy and well-reined animalism; I am seeking to disentangle the popular admiration for "French taste" from the mists of glamour and false sentiment by which it has been surrounded, and this can only be done effectually if we carefully examine its springs of action, and test them at the fountain-head,—(for Paris is the fountain-head, beyond all doubt).

It requires the *abandon* possessed by the French to dare to originate such fashions, and to be the first to wear them; and I have gone at some length into a question which can only parenthetically belong to this treatise, because I believe that this insane race after French fashions forms one of the great obstacles in the way of attaining a true "taste"—of having a simple and wholesome judgment in the design and colour of our clothes, our furniture, our trifles of luxury and ease. And if I have shown that the stream is impure from the fountain that French taste does not flow from a love of beautiful things for beauty's sake, but through a love of fashion and display aroused quite irrespectively of true taste, and only from a desire of public *éclat*—we may well look askance at all such matters coming from France, and not be surprised if we find that they have trampled upon every law of the beautiful.

I cannot, of course, forget that a large proportion of women are happily too modest and too sensible to accept extreme French fashions. Some refuse them altogether, and a still larger number tone them down to suit their own sense of what is decorous and becoming; but in considering the effect of "Fashion" upon society, it is instructive to observe the very wide extent to which the fashion of partial nudity of the arms and bust has been followed among women who are otherwise perfectly modest, and in coteries only quite moderately fashionable.

But fashions and novelties of dress gain their hold on us unfairly as it were, evade our critical powers, and obtain a hold upon us through our lower senses.

Women are beyond doubt the decorative and pleasurable side of life, so to speak; the lights and ornaments of our homes; and it is not only their interest but their duty to present themselves to us in the most interesting and attractive manner possible, so long as that manner be consistent with a modesty originally supplied by that deep and innate leaning towards chastity, which only the most gross and corrupt eras in society have ever broken down. Now, when a comely and attractive woman, desiring to look her best, and conscious perhaps of personal beauty, of symmetry of figure, of grace of carriage, presents herself before us, even in an extreme Parisian fashion, in which she feels no immodesty because she knows that "Society" has endorsed her costume, our critical faculties as to the art of her dress are not called into action, in fact, are hoodwinked and hustled away—the appeal is to our affections—our judgment is taken by storm; the *tout ensemble* is pronounced good, and once more up goes the acclaim in favour of "French taste."

But the very foremost axioms of good taste may have been defied a hundred times in the process, and colours and patterns may have been tolerated for their novelty which even a modist of experience must know to be utterly bad, when judged by any sound standard.

It may be useful here to notice two very prominent examples exhibiting French design in its true colours, because in each we may fairly argue that the designer is in sober earnest and not merely running after novelty in playful caprice.

Who that is familiar with the external aspect of an English country-house, inartistic for the most part, but unpretentious, much altered, and rejoicing in its lack of symmetry, quaintly defiant of architectural proprieties, radiant in its jessamine and ivy and roses, and half-hidden in evergreens, can fail to be struck by the rather appalling spectacle of a modern French house. With the design of a biscuit-box set up on end, with the flattest of roofs, always hipped—the very meanest kind of roof conceivable—rejoicing in sharply defined and conspicuous quoins at all the angles and openings, the intervening spaces being often plastered and whitewashed—intentionally kept clear of climbing plants, and holding itself up perkly and conceited, ostentatiously pretentious, it forms an object in the landscape only somewhat more hideous than those lopped and untree-like trees with which it is surrounded.

Mr. Ruskin has well said, that if a nation may anywhere be supposed to be entirely serious and in earnest, it is in its graveyards and memorials to its dead. Go to a modern French cemetery, and you find uglinesses which it has surely been reserved for the French alone to invent and find delight in. To mention two only: the most approved form of memorial cross is a sort of cast-iron skeleton, a fanciful open trellis affair, losing sight of the whole idea and nature of the Cross of Calvary; and this they paint black and white to make it "telling". The old "immortelle" wreath of yellow gnaphalium was at least pleasant and suggestive; but modern French craving for novelty has cast it aside, and substituted a "wreath" of beads set on wire, at once losing the ring-like form, and so the emblematical value; its centre filled with foolish sentimental legends also done in beads and wire, and forming altogether one of the most hideous things on earth. Anyone rejoicing in "French taste" should pay a visit to the statuary shops in the street leading to Pere la Chaise: those in our own Euston Road are not exhilarating, but these have the smell of the charnel house and the imbecility of the lunatic asylum marvellously combined.

In so large a range of industries carried on by a nation of fifty millions of very industrious and clever people, it would be wonderful indeed if there were no exceptions to any rule we might prove to prevail; and, curiously enough, the French are great admirers of Oriental art, and good copiers of it (on account, perhaps, of its piquancy and novelty to them); but with this and some other exceptions, French "taste" is utterly and wholly corrupt and bad, both in essence and in end, and it exercises the worst possible influence on the aesthetic perceptions of both Europe and America.

It will be replied, perhaps, "Ah, but much of the so-called 'French taste' you see, crude and staring, inharmonious and conspicuous, is not really French, but is an English travesty. We get French fashions, and, copying them without their dexterity, vulgarise and denigrate them." This is probably very true about a large proportion of articles of women's dress made in this country after French fashion-books; but how about the things actually sent from France—the magenta and "night green," and "Aniline" violet silks and ribbons, the chintzes and muslins, the china and bronzes? It will not be denied that these truly exhibit what could be called French "taste". It is also undeniable that it is from France, principally, that we get the detestable fashion which has set in of late years for loading our sitting-rooms with all manner of useless, showy, and tricky trifles of no manner of use whatever, and giving them a fussy and fidgety aspect, which is, to a rightly ordered mind, exasperating. Not only must the backs of chairs have fancy towels—knotted and otherwise—but even flower-pots must be draped, the very earth the plant grows in must be hidden by silk; while the table is crowded with innumerable objects, worthless, useless, and disturbing. And as if this was not enough, the wall must be bedizened with photographs in fancy frames, accompanied, more or less, by a quantity of ribbon. The top of the dado is increased until it becomes a stand for all sorts of abominations; and every available space, the tops of cabinets, little side tables, shelves below those tables, &c., must be crowded with fancy rubbish; not to mention sham easels, imitation bee-hives, straw hats, and other ridiculous nonsense, which are not only distressing to the general effect, but are exceedingly cumbrous to those who want to move about in the room, and are being continually swept out of their places by the dresses of the occupants.

The fidgety unrest produced in such rooms, and tolerated, not to say enjoyed, by their owners, indicates strikingly the deterioration of taste which set the rubbish in its place. Nothing but "Fashion" could have made such an exhibition possible. No love of the beautiful for beauty's sake could have brought into existence the fussy little table covered over with silver trinkets; which, it must be confessed, is the least objectionable of all these modern fashions. Indeed, this deterioration having once set in, there is nothing which is impossible: the victims will go to the length of any folly which is supposed to be fashionable.

Truly this is a bad school for the education of our taste; and improvement is scarcely possible with such surroundings.

An escape into the garden, the wood, and the field must somehow be secured: for there Nature can be studied. For it is to Nature we must look for relief from such rubbish, and for a standard of beauty besides. Much may be done, no doubt, in the study, the picture-gallery, the museum, to produce a healthy tone in the imagination so afflicted; but Nature is the better school; and those who will patiently study the sky, the hills, the woods, the foliage, the flowers, will find there their best anodyne. It is not necessary for this purpose to go to Scotland, or to Switzerland, or to the Andes. Let the student take the nearest hedgerow out of reach of the modern row of villas, and he will find abundant study before him. Let him learn to understand the beauty of a bank of wild thyme with its apparently violent contrast of bright green and bright red, and how it becomes possible for such contrast to become beautiful, through that infinite power of gradation which Nature alone can show him. To learn from whence arises the beauty and charm of the azalea leaf or the columbine, or even the foliage of the humble carrot after the first autumn frosts, will be a lesson that cannot be taught by books. It may then become possible for him to find delight nearer home, in the foliage of sea-kale, or even of the friendly cabbage. A new door will be open to him for fresh beauties in Nature, always existing, but seen now with another pair of eyes; and, if the physiologists tell us true, enjoyed with fresh cells of the brain, which have been formed for the purpose. The museum, the picture-gallery, the sculpture-room may follow; and if we must still go to France, let it be to the Louvre. In time there may be a chance for the patient and careful student to learn beauty for its own sake, and to produce, according to the degree of natural aptitude he or she may possess, a delightful "taste," which shall be a joy forever.

Chapter 3
Beauty in Form and Colour

~⋘✦⋙~

What do we mean by beauty? A sensation of delight, resulting from the fitness and completeness of a picture which is offered to the eye, the ear, or the mind? It maybe Nature, or Art, or a poetical idea, music, what not? The field is wide, and ever widening. Beyond doubt, our forerunners of even sixty years ago regarded mountains, rocky hills, and uncultivated ground as "cruel" and "horrid." We, on the contrary (thanks, perhaps, to Sir Walter Scott), regard them as beautiful; so that the remark, "Beauty is in the eye of the beholder," contains more truth than one at first perceives. Moreover, the power to appreciate beauty truly arises from the education of the faculties, so that in endeavouring to define what we mean by "beauty," we must presuppose some culture. But that is no reason for doubting the existence of a real standard of beauty. India is no less our possession because there are outlying fringes which are not definitely under our rule. Indeed, the very fact of that doubtful ownership of these outlying parts is of itself a proof of the admitted ownership of the rest.

Nothing can be a greater mistake than to try and decide a question of beauty by quoting the well-known phrase, "It is a question of taste." This is merely a weak endeavour to shirk the complex and intricate questions at issue, and reveals the fact that most people do not care to face them, and would even like to make it appear that there is no such thing as a standard of beauty at all.

It is extremely easy, in a matter of this sort, to puzzle each other, and to make hedges of paradox behind which disputants may retreat.

"Why is olive green a more serviceable colour than emerald green?" asks one. "Why is not mauve admissible as a colour for a wall?" asks another. A third says, "How can you admire Italian decorative art in the face of German?" We might say, relatively speaking, that Westminster Abbey is beautiful, but that St. Pancras Railway Station is ugly. Whereupon someone replies, "But is St. Pancras Station ugly? And if Westminster Abbey is beautiful, and Gothic architecture most suitable for a religious building, how do you come to admire St. Paul's?" And there are a thousand other such questions; to which the average citizen replies, "It is a question of taste, and there is no disputing about taste."

Nothing can be more untrue and misleading, for it means (if it means anything at all) that there is no true standard of right or wrong in such matters; that many men judging differently on one subject, are *all* right—clearly a paradox. A bad doctrine indeed, and false all through. For it assumes that they are equally competent to judge; that their tastes have been equally educated; moreover, that they *are* educated, having had opportunity to read widely and to study their subject. If they had had these advantages, then their diversity of opinion might be interesting and instructive; but the adage, as at present used, would not imply that at all. In an ignorant and illogical time it might pass muster for a while; but we seem to have arrived, in the world's history, at a period when accurate (that is to say, scientific) reasons for most things are not only demanded, but, for the most part, to be had; and even Art questions must be treated with more scientific exactness. A woman's reason, "I like it because I like it," will no longer suffice.

Of course Mr. Ruskin, in his "Seven Lamps," "Modern Painters," and "Stones of Venice" has said much, and said it nobly, upon this subject; but his books alone are quite beyond the average reader, and, besides, are full of an empiricism which ruffles a good many students, and renders short extracts from his books impossible. If you read them all through, you arrive at the conclusion that their author knows emi-nently well what he is talking about, and that be ultimately gives rea-sons for all his statements, but it is done in a form which defies the "skipping" reader, and renders quotations all but impossible, unless you are quoting to his scholars and admirers.

To such apparently puzzling questions as I have alluded, short an-swers cannot be given, unless they be excessively empirical; and then, to many minds, they seem no answer at all. "You *must* like it" —"you *ought* to like it"—"it is fine colour"—"it is 'noble form' "—"the verdict of the ages is in its favour," &c. Someone of course will start up, men-tally or actually, and assert: "How do we know but that the verdict of the ages may be wrong? I am afraid I cannot merely accept your state-ment on it."

Now, it is especially worthy of remark, on the threshold of the subject, that in these questions, where apparently the eyesight is mainly consulted, people are most confident in their own judgment, however uncultivated, and most impatient of control.

If a man of average education gets drawn into conversation about literature or music, he will hold his tongue when it comes to pro-nouncing judgment, seeing plainly that precise, or "scientific," knowl-edge is required before he can speak with credit to himself. But in regard to pictorial art, a very large proportion of people consider that their own eyes are sufficient to guide them to admire what is good, and to eschew the contrary. There are numbers of educated people who are as ignorant of Art as they are of Nature, who never open a book upon any such subject, who will yet go to the Royal Academy or the Louvre, and pronounce judgment right and left with an assur-ance, and apparent familiarity, which should only belong to the most experienced of experts. They think their eyesight is qualification enough.

Nothing could be a greater mistake; such seeing is a mere animal instinct, as a rabbit sees a terrier and bolts.

The reason of this mistake is not very evident. To be sure, literature demands a great deal of hard reading, and a pretender is quickly found out; while music keeps the ignorant at a respectful distance by the mere difficulty of deciphering it. But it is not clear why people are cautious about confessing that they like dance-music, and find a Monday "Pop." very tedious, and are yet not at all afraid of declaring that they prefer the Royal Academy to the National Gallery; further than this, that vulgar opinion on the subject holds much study and hard work as necessary for a knowledge of literature or music, but only a pair of eyes for art. Beyond doubt, but for the necessity, widely felt among people, who desire above all things to be in good "form," for speaking with caution, and even with some show of reverence, about things held sacred in museums and picture-galleries, which have manifestly received the favourable verdict of the ages, a large majority would confess their entire indifference, or even active dislike, to *old* art, so strenuous is its demand upon something more than mere eyesight for its right understanding. From the point of view of mere animal eyesight they can scarcely bear to look at it.

Beyond doubt, we have to *learn to see*. No one ever *quite* sees a landscape until he has learnt to draw one; no one ever truly sees the beauty of flowers until he has tried to represent them—their exquisite forms and subtle gradations; or, what is not so pleasant, pulled them to pieces, and put them under the microscope. No one knows the everlasting hills till he has learned something of their geology, of the action of water in their ravines, of the action of ice in bygone ages—of their history, in fact.

All this shows that the information ordinarily passed to the brain by the eyes of those who have not specially studied the subject we are at present discussing, is quite incomplete and untrustworthy. It may guide us satisfactorily in the choice of a salad or a partridge for dinner, or to distinguish between a genuine Bank of England note and a note of the "Bank of Elegance," but it is wholly inadequate to help us to discriminate between good and bad colour, or base and noble form.

So that the majority of people, trusting to mere animal eyesight and mother-wit, and not having time or inclination to correct and amplify these by exact knowledge, acquire early in life bad habits of eyesight, feeble or diseased views of Nature and Art, which stick to them through life, and operate automatically, without special thought or action of the intellect; they only half-see anything, and that half they see badly. Indeed, more; the eye, having become accustomed to bad colour and form, insensibly goes down the hill and demands something worse and more stimulating; or, finding no great interest in such things at all, gives up even troubling itself with their existence, and settles down content with dull commonplace, without thought or desire.

In the use of the eyes, then, no less than in matters of the appetite, man may be described as a machine apt to go wrong; and just as we need instruction and guidance with regard to the finer details of conduct, and counsels of watchfulness and temperance for our appetites, so do we need all these to teach us how to *see* aright.

Distrust, therefore, first impressions of all visible objects; for even in the late summer and autumn of life, when we may have learned a good deal, mature and reconsidered judgment is still the safest. Nor should second or final impressions be considered of value until the subject has been well studied, and the scholar has learned at least how little he knows.

And not only may we acquire, through imperfect education, or early association, habits of thought, taste, and eyesight which are misleading and mischievous, but we may fall into a mode of life which renders us less and less competent to perceive and assimilate impressions of beauty. The man who spends his day in the drudgery of his office, snatches what breathless time he can over his mid-day chop for the perusal of the daily paper, comes home worn out, and has no inclination for anything after dinner but the billiard-table or the chatter of his club smoking-room, is not very much in the way of acquiring correct notions about the treasures at South Kensington, the Louvre, or the Vatican, especially if on the few days he can snatch from business he devotes his time to undiluted Epsom or Newmarket, to the cuisine of foreign hotels, or the folly of the "day off," where the "form" of the turn-out, and of the girls, and the dryness of the champagne, are the foremost and all-absorbing topics of conversation.

But this is preamble; only the outlines of so wide a subject can be touched; and if we have spent too much time on scaffolding, we are no worse off than those excellent French builders who, when they have a house to build, first put up a crane high enough and far-reaching enough to raise the complete edifice.

First, let us consider Beauty of Colour. Nature must be our textbook, though we must not for one moment suppose that the colouring of Nature, and of Art, can ever be thought of as identical. We will return to this question further on; meanwhile it may be sufficient to bear in mind how much shorter is the gamut of colour possible in Art (this does not occur to the ordinary reader or student, but the fact can easily be tested. Compare white paper with white clouds in high light, or a board painted black with the shadows cast by the mid-day sun); nevertheless, we can only turn to Nature for authority and text.

What we want above all things is *temperance*. "Temperance," says Mr. Ruskin, "is the power that governs energy, and in respect of things prone to excess it regulates the quantity." Now, Nature is always *temperate*. I do not forget that she has produced malachite, the bell-gentian, the sunflower; I do not forget the existence of many tropical flowers of great brilliancy—the *Speciosissimus cactus*, for instance; but with regard to this and similar plants of great showiness, it should be borne in mind, first, for how short a time this great brilliancy lasts —five or six days at most out of three hundred and sixty-five; and secondly, what a moderate area there is of this gorgeous colour mea-

sured against the greens and greys and browns of the surrounding
vegetation. But even in the case of the very gayest flowering plant
ever seen, a careful examination will reveal the fact that what to the
careless observer seemed a blaze of a certain tint, is in reality a mass
of subtle gradations—of which more presently.

A gorgeous sunset lasts but a few minutes out of the twenty-four
hours, and is, even then, generally small in area compared with the
whole arc of the heavens; and it is so full of gradations, that observers
argue, after it is gone, whether it was chiefly red, or chiefly yellow, or
purple, orange, or grey.

A field of spring grass, especially after thunder-rain, often seems
dazzlingly brilliant; but sit down and try to draw it. There is one colour—emerald green—in an ordinary paint-box which, if you can use
it at all, you must use in such small particles as at once to proclaim
its unnatural crudity; and yet this is the colour that is selected in all
its untoned fierceness by our educated gentry for lining their billiard-
tables, and by our neighbours, the French, for painting their shutters.
But in this grass-field you will find infinite and perplexing gradations,
such as you cannot follow with the brush, such as you can only hint
at; the shadow of one blade lying on the next, one glossy in high light,
the next half-coloured only, and in shade; and if it should happen that
you have in your pocket some of the blue or green paper bands used
round envelopes, or some patterns of silk or merino from a shop, you
will be astonished at their crudity and fierceness compared with the
softness and gradations of Nature.

A student of colour soon finds out that beauty of colour begins with
gradation, that the loveliness of graduated colour is so great that,
relatively, level colour is not beautiful at all; but he also finds out that
there is no such thing as level colour in Nature—natural colour is
always in a state of gradation.

How many of us, having ideally schemed the colour of the walls or
woodwork of a room, and having set the painter to work, have felt

utterly chilled and disappointed at the result, have accused the workman of a "bad match," and when he proves that this is not so, we have turned away, puzzled and sick of the matter. It is because the painter has been straining every effort to give you a perfectly even colour, and we have felt instinctively that it was *bad* colour.

Nature teems with gradations. For example, let me take the case of the bell-gentian, which, at first glance, seems about as crude a piece of violent colour as we can think of. This is a good flower to choose, because artists and decorators all know that a crude and violent blue is of all colours the most difficult to deal with. Do not let us say a *bad* colour, because it is as incorrect to speak of any colour as "bad," as it would be to speak of arsenic, for instance, as a bad drug. Let us say a difficult drug or colour to deal with, one where a little will go a long way; for both powder blue and arsenic may, each in turn, be both necessary and desirable.

Let us try to examine a gentian in detail.

If a slit be cut a quarter of an inch wide, in a piece of cardboard, divided down its centre by a fine thread, and a scale of eighths of inches marked down the sides, so that laying another card across the slit, and moving it downwards an eighth of an inch at a time, small squares of one-eighth of an inch each way are successively exposed, these may then be examined and catalogued. The slit should pass twice across the brilliant lip of the flower, and across the centre or bell, and then down the outside of the bell to the calyx. It will be observed that we take no notice at present of the green leaves, though these are an important factor in the general effect, as one sees a mass of flowers growing.

The colour of the tiny squares is seldom even approximately the same over its whole area, so that we are driven to give each square the value of four, and catalogue it as, say, 2 brilliant blue, 1 dark blue, 1 purple; and by this subdivision we arrive at a total of 120 units.

Not to weary the reader with dry detail, let us come at once to the result. Of the gaudy powder blue tint we cannot find so much as one-fourth of the whole; but, of the same colour much deeper, one-eighth, and of purplish blue—no doubt quite as brilliant in its effect on the eye as the other two—one-sixteenth.

Still, in this startlingly blue flower, not one-half is coloured as a careless observer would suppose the whole to be. We next come to one-sixth of blue, so dark as to be only distinguishable from black in a strong light; and the remaining colours may be called bluish-grey-black, dirty bluish-green, greyish indigo, dark and light, and actual apple-green, in spots a little way down the bell; so that, roughly speaking, this brilliantly blue flower is not half blue.

The exceeding blueness of a gentian arises from the fact that all these greyish and partially blue and green tints *lead up* to the fierce blue of the lip; it is a splendid instance of the force of gradation, the blueness of the blue being all the bluer to our eyes, because of the dulness of the other tints—a dulness, however, which is leading us up to the key-note, blue.

We thus learn that Nature, even when she plays high, does so with a splendid moderation. But a lady who has made up her mind to a bright blue dress buys the whole quantity of that one tint.

Let us now take another and quite a different case—the red mullet — perhaps the loveliest piece of colour to be found, after an opal;—but then the opal will not lend itself to examination as a dead mullet will. We all see mullets as rosy and tempting morsels on the fishmonger's stall, but those who will take the trouble to examine one, will find it a wonderfully complex and gorgeous piece of colouring. While it exhibits the power of gradation in Nature as perfectly as a gentian, they will find that it arrives at its splendour in a totally different way. The rosiest part of the fish is across the middle, a little nearer the tail than the head; but the loveliest and most brilliant colour is generally nearer the head.

Adopting the same system of examination as before, we arrive at eighth-inch squares of the value of 4, as before, and total units 260. This excludes 32 units of glistening white, in which no colour at all is discoverable.

Of very pale pink, full pink, deep pink, rich red, crimson, flame colour, and scarlet, all telling upon the eye as rosy reds, not more than 98 out of 260 could be discovered, or somewhat more than one-third; next, one-tenth of the whole in straw-colour and full gold (enhancing and leading up to the red, no doubt). But this is altogether, observe, less than one-half of the colouring of this red fish.

Next, about one-thirteenth of primula, or deep purplish red. Primula, of course, is rich red tinged with blue, a colour not leading up to reds, but neutralising their redness. If we hand over half of this to the red part of the catalogue, we arrive at a trifle more than one half (134½ / 260ths). After this, all the colouring of our bright red fish tells the other way; not detracting from its colour, but very much from its redness—blues, greens, cold purples, olives, and greys (plus 32 white, *nil*).

To be sure, the pinks and golds are, for the most part, rich and powerful, and the other colours are thin and watery; still, remember we are measuring areas, not depths of effect.

But while granting this modification, is it not wonderful to find that the remaining tints of this red fish arrange themselves thus blues, greens, and cold purples, 78; olives and greys, 37; and adding to these the cold half of the primula, we arrive at 125½ / 260ths, or very nearly one-half, of tints which do not go to make red at all, but actually detract from it?

In making studies of many beautiful coloured things—flowers, iridescence on pigeons' necks and shells, peacocks' feathers, fresh mackerel, and many other such things—one never comes upon a piece of brilliant colour which is not bewildering and puzzling by the complexity with which harmonious and even opposing colours interlace and fade into each other. On the other hand, it is well worthy of notice that some natural objects, manifestly less attractive than others, as, for instance, the foliage of the common laurel, are found, on examination, not to be ungraduated, but feeble and monotonous (comparatively speaking) in their gradations.

Thus, we learn two lessons in colour:

First: Natural colour is always in gradation.

Second: Natural colour is always temperate. I propose to avoid quasi-scientific details: as to what colours are primary and what secondary, nobody is agreed, and it does not matter. But you will readily understand that when I speak of crude blue I mean something like washerwomen's powder blue. Crude green means what we often see in a German toy or a newly-painted Venetian blind; peacock blue, magenta, and strong aniline purple, are all crude colours; and that distinction will serve our purpose better than phrases about which people quarrel. Now, if we want to paint the wall of a room, or buy a dress, and for good reasons desire a red effect, and for sundry reasons, also good, find it impossible to use six or eight graduating tints, we must certainly avoid a brilliant magenta or crimson, because it would be, first, ungraduated, and, second, intemperate. Nature would probably have used a little magenta in combination with other and softer tints, but we are debarred by time, expense, and other considerations. What are we to do? Let us go to Nature, and see how she manages. Let us take careful note of the relative proportions of bright red, quiet dirty red, grey, brown, and faded tints, and mix our paint or dye accordingly. We shall probably arrive at a colour something between bricks and leather—a good, useful, pleasant colour, nice to live with, and hurting the feelings of nobody; restful to the eye, and leaving a healthy appetite for red mullets, and other beautiful and brilliant reds, in Nature or fine art.

And having thus learned a practical lesson from Nature, we should fearlessly stick to it; and in time we shall come to appreciate the value of quiet, moderate, tertiary tints.

We should always doubt all amazingly attractive, coloured things of human manufacture; and when the standard has thus been kept up for some years, we become conscious of a refined taste in colour, and can then revel in the colour of Nature, and in that of fine art also, whether it comes from the hand of Titian or Tintoretto, Orchardson or Clara Montalba. And, as our perceptions strengthen, we find ourselves out of love with even pale and moderate colour, if it be level and without gradation; the lumpy bottom of a green glass bottle becomes at once a source of pleasure, where none is given by the thin even tint of the bottle itself.

The eye becomes critical, and sees a new charm both in Nature and Art, and appreciates "*fine colour*;" colour, not only temperate and in gradation, but in intricate and gorgeous intermingling of splendid tints, such as one sees in the plumage of Oriental birds and butterflies —gold peering through crimson and flame—green and coppery mosses on grey rocks, or a portrait of Titian's, bronzy green velvet with gold braiding, against rosy flesh tints. A bit of fine colour becomes more precious than diamonds; old, faded Italian silks of more value than new ones; old Indian rugs, stained and worn, better than any modern carpet. Our tastes become susceptible of offence about things that before seemed indifferent, and though it will always be a comfort to a man's wife that his shirts and table-linen should be snow-white, ivory seems white enough for anything, and in decorative work, whitey-brown paper is the best white there is.

There are not a few people, desirous above all things that their surroundings should be in the highest taste, who are feverishly anxious and uneasy as to whether things will "go with" sundry other things, having mostly in their minds a fearful list of things which will not "go with" each other. Terra-cotta reds must not come near greeny blues—especially not near crimsony reds; reds of any sort do not "go with" greens and blues, &c. &c., and so on, and so on, *ad lib*.

Now, it is worthy of notice that if one goes into the garden to gather a posy, a piece of house-decoration which some folk perform almost daily, one gathers flowers, as a rule, without any idea of what will "go with" each other, but simply the flowers that happen to be blowing, and of the right dimensions for the proposed posy; and, ninety-nine times out of a hundred, the flowers so gathered "go with" each other delightfully. Why, then, should people be so nervous as to whether the proposed carpet will "go with" the proposed curtains? Clearly because the colour of one, or both, is bad—crude, violent, or without gradation; and because, while the posy is well mingled with green and grey and neutral tints, the carpet and curtains are wholly or partially deficient in these.

If anyone wants to try whether this is a practical fact, let him buy or borrow a really fine old Persian carpet, which will probably contain blues and greens, reds and yellows, orange, quiet purples, and whites of various degrees, in fact, almost as many colours as the garden posy, and he will find that the chances are enormously in favour of its looking well in any room in which he may throw it down, with an entire disregard for what may be already there.

And, upon examination, it will be found that such a carpet, however gay it may look, will contain no crude or ungraduated colour whatever. Not only will its blue ground, for instance, prove to be made up, intentionally, of four or five blues, but each thread will be found to be similarly composed, perhaps without intention—a circumstance probably due to the Oriental habit of mixing various sorts of wool and hair, or at least all the qualities of each; while our spinners and dyers strain every nerve to make each fibre exactly match its fellows.

Take care that each colour, in each article you buy, be soft, and graduated, and free from crudity, and then you may set them all together and be happy.

To turn for a moment to Form. As gradation is the condition of beauty in colour, so curvature is the ground of all loveliness in form.

I do not suppose anyone will question this, because no one pretends to find beauty in an office ruler or a dahlia stick; and if we see a very straight and unbending young woman, we say "she has swallowed a poker."

Curvature is the groundwork of beauty, but temperance again is the ruling power. It would, of course, take far too long to analyse ever so slightly that touchstone of all beautiful curvature, the human form; but if anyone wishes to see how severely temperate nature is, let him obtain a drawing of the human arm, and see how strenuously slight are the deviations from straight lines, and he will find also that the rest of the body of a young and healthy person is throughout of this character.

One may find a hundred examples from Nature of this strenuously restrained curvature. One thinks of the leaves of holly and herberis as a multitude of exceedingly sharp and quickly rounded curves; but a careful examination shows them to be practically squares, with quite little points added for prickles, and the space between prickle and prickle is very nearly a straight line—very nearly, but not quite.

The alder leaf is practically a pentagon with the angles pared off a little, and only a little. A willow leaf is a collection of nearly straight lines, with delicate little curves at each end. An oleander leaf is still more severe, and many aspects of it are all but straight lines. And the more one examines forms of this sort, the more one sees that vigorously restrained curvature is, in its restraint, the groundwork of beauty in form.

To consider then the bearing of these facts on the choice of pictures, stained glass, wall decorations, furniture, cabinet ornaments, carpets, and curtains, all the hundred odds and ends of our house; and last, but by no means least, dress. But this is a wide field, and, for practical purposes, may be narrowed down to the questions of wall decoration and patterned objects generally; for these are, as it were, central in the group, and likely to throw light upon the others.

To clear the ground before we begin to build, let it be taken as an axiom with the utmost distinctness, that we must never look upon copies of Nature, however accurate they be, as anything more than the alphabet and primer for the artist and decorator—an alphabet very necessary, in fact the only alphabet for the purpose, and absolutely indispensable, but only an alphabet or primer after all; the building materials, but never, under any circumstances, the building; the means, but not the end.

To take a practical instance, let us suppose that a gardener produces a new red rose, and that horticulturists agree to call it the Acme rose. The grower is naturally proud of it, and he employs Mrs. Allingham, for instance, to make a drawing of it. If she does it well, the matter is passing into the realms of art. But the grower is not content; he calls on Shannon, for instance, to take a portrait of his wife holding the rose in her hand, or a spray of these roses across her bosom. We have now got into fine art. This is such a success that he wants these roses all over his drawing-room wall, and he goes, or would a few weeks ago have gone, to that master of art decoration, now, alas, at rest from his helpful labours, William Morris, and said, "Decorate me these walls with my Acme rose." "Well, but," Morris would have replied, "this won't do; your walls would be all over red dots. Besides, I can't give you all these lovely details at any price that a sensible man would pay. I must simplify it, and moderate your reds and greens. I must also get rid of a quantity of light and shade, and flatten it, so to speak."

Supposing it well done, we have passed downwards from fine art to decorative art. But the rose-grower wants to carry the thing a step further—he wants his rose as a decoration for a dinner-service, and he goes to Wedgwood. "Well," says Wedgwood, "but we must get this rose pattern into a condition which ordinary draughtsmen and printers and potters can deal with; we must reduce it to one or two tints, and simplify it further even than Morris did."

So we arrive, by a certain process, at flat, conventional patterning. In the earlier part of our argument, we arrived at the sheer necessity of using quiet, tertiary tints where gradation of colour was unattainable "at the money." Thus, the Acme rose pattern has arrived, inevitably, at flat formality of outline and greys, or only suggestions of green and red in colour, while sense of projection has disappeared entirely.

Broadly, in *fine art*, there are no limits to the legitimate representation of form, projection, colour, but those necessarily incidental to all the works of man viewed in relation to Nature. But as you come down in the scale, stained glass, painted frieze, brocaded silk, wall paper, striped cotton print, the limitations become many and severe, by sheer necessity, and apart from questions of taste, and to refuse to bow to them indicates stupidity and blindness. Temperance steps in, and enjoins moderation and simplicity in curvature, gradation and sobriety in colour you have admitted the axioms, accept the result.

Moreover, the limitations in fine art, which we have called incidental to all the works of man, are in reality very considerable; for, firstly, the most skilful eye and hand the world has known could never reproduce the intricate and overwhelming detail of the colours of Nature, not to mention subtleties of minute form. And even if we were not thus limited (which under favourable circumstances might conceivably be the case), there remains, secondly, the fact already alluded to, viz., that the gamut or scale of art is far shorter, both in light and shade and in colour, than that of Nature.

No white paint or paper can approach the whiteness of a cloud illumined by sunshine, and no black paint is as dark as the shadow, say, of a tree thrown by strong sunlight against a pale grey limestone wall. The bluest paint is a feeble thing compared with the azure of the heavens; and though some pigments are too fierce for our imperfect handling, seeing that we cannot follow the delicacy of Nature's gradations, yet at every turn the student of Nature finds tints in nature too dazzling for reproduction. He has only, therefore, humbly to follow his guide at a respectful distance; and, just as we say one had better not bark if he cannot bite, so the accomplished artist finds out what he can do and what he had better avoid. He begins to understand what is possible in paint on canvas; and partly by the experience of the past, and partly by the light of his own perceptions, he recognises the limits of his art, and arranges his scale of colour and light and shade in accordance with those limits. And so, gradually but inevitably, colouring in art has arrived at a condition which, originally framed on that of Nature, has come to the average observer to appear wholly distinct.

To put the matter into the most practical form. We all know the beautiful metallic blue butterfly from South America, *Cypromorpho* by name. Let us suppose that a lover of realism desires to have this most lovely creature well copied, and that a copyist with a good eye for colour, and the touch of an Oriental, takes the utmost pains to accomplish it—that he works on a ground of silver, in the purest Prussian blue—it is conceivable that a very admirable, realistic representation might be produced.

It is now desired, let us suppose, to introduce it as a detail into a picture. But it is quickly discovered that this is impossible materials and pigments do not exist with which we can copy other brilliant objects in an equivalent manner, and it is perceived that if they did nobody could bear the result; for the blue butterfly already painted stands out as a flaring spot, like an electric light at a railway station; and thus two insurmountable barriers declare that the attempt must be given up. It is not a question of *degree*, it is one of *kind*. Where is the loose screw? In the mistake made by a large number of people in supposing that art is a *copy of Nature*. A copy of Nature (as much of a copy, that is, as the human eye and hand are capable of) may be a stepping-stone or handmaid to Art, a scaffolding on which to stand while building; but never, as we have mentioned before, the building —Art itself.

True Art is a *representation* of Nature; and a representation, to be true and good, must be such as to produce in the mind of the spectator sensations fairly equivalent to those produced by Nature herself.

And here steps in the creative faculty of the artist. He perceives the enormous difference in the conditions. The blue butterfly, dancing with his fellows in the light of a southern sun, surrounded by leagues of soft atmosphere, by greys and blues of distance, and greens and browns of forest and fell, is one thing; the blue butterfly pinned on a cork in a studio, with a background of drapery or canvas, is quite another, and to confound them is unpardonable muddling. There is no southern sunshine or any other sunshine in the studio; the scale of possible colour falls far short of the top, and finishes far above the bottom; the whole thing must be altered and arranged to suit the altered conditions, and, with the rearrangement, the silver ground and most of the Prussian blue disappears.

And all this applies as truly, in degree, to good decorative work as to high art, and as much to form as to colour.

Those who have gone through the course of study from Nature indicated by these remarks, may continue their education at museums and picture-galleries. Here are the great treasures of the past which will form the best of all schools, and here they can study a fresh chapter of their subject, the difference, namely, between noble and ignoble form between what is elevating in motive, and what is base and degrading; and we shall constantly find that the painters who offend in this respect are precisely those whose colour is violent, and whose form is wanting in restraint. South Kensington is an infinite treasure-house to learn in, and to think about in after years. We should go there continually. Our own National Gallery, the Louvre, and Florence, it need not be said, may complete the studies, and even help us to understand and appreciate such painters as Giotto, Cimabue, Andrea del Sarto, and Botticelli.

But in daily life let us avoid all ugly and crude colours, and base and ignoble subjects, as we avoid bad smells; and when we go to a fresh place let us make at once for the Parish Church, if it be an old one. For the tight grip in which the earning of our daily bread holds most of us, so commonly prevents our visiting museums and picture-galleries as often as we ought, that we may find ourselves shut up among the base and dull and ignoble things, like offices, and railway stations, and hotels, for months together. So, whenever there is a chance to get, even for a quarter of an hour, among objects of noble intention, or possible beauty of form and colour, we should eagerly seize it. Now, old architecture will always be found to have some element of beauty in it shaft or arch or bit of carving, stained glass, old woodwork, or sculptured tomb; and we may get more real pleasure and profit out of a habit of making for the "old church," than out of all the theatres, drapers' and jewellers' shops, hotel dinners, and picnic parties which we have ever seen or ever can see.

It is worthy of remark, that in stained glass—quite the most beautiful form of decorative art—we have all agreed, for generations past, not to be hindered by the very severe limitations and conditions under which the artist has to work; and I suppose no one ever thought of ordering a stained-glass window to be done to "Nature."

We recognise the propriety of strong lines round many forms which we know do not exist in Nature; we are satisfied that a distinguished person should have a glory, like a dinner-plate, round the head, and that the whole work should be permeated by broad (lead) lines of black—lines which no one of experience ever dreams of trying to dispense with.

Sir Joshua Reynolds, in the Chapel of King's, Cambridge, endeavoured to get rid of these lines, and his failure is a warning to us all to keep clear of such realistic experiments in decorative work.

With trifling exceptions, *old "classic" art must always be preferable to modern art, at least for this generation and the next.*

And if we were asked to assign a reason for such a formidable a statement, we should reply that no one who has seen, with his eyes open, such a collection of fine and decorative art as that at South Kensington, can be unaware of the marvellous superiority of the work handed down to us from the fourteenth to the seventeenth centuries (putting Greek art out of the question for the moment), in pictures, in sculpture, in wall decorations, in embroidery, in ironwork, in pottery—in all departments indeed of fine and decorative art that the men of those centuries put their hands to. No painter of this day pretends for one moment that any man alive can paint as well as Michael Angelo, Raphael, Titian, and many other Italians; no Staffordshire potter, or any other potter elsewhere, pretends or maintains that he can produce anything equal to the best lustre-ware of mediaeval Italy—and so it is through all these arts.

We ask why? The answer is, that art was then *traditional*; that is to say, a painter or handicraftsman was brought up to the craft of his father and grandfather, and simply and naturally produced the article he had been taught to produce from boyhood. And so it came to pass that, in the centuries I have alluded to, Europe was full of young men trained from boyhood to their respective crafts; it was their pride to carry on the family tradition, and it was the delight of the wealthy soldier, statesman, ecclesiastic, or burgher to vie with each other in buying their wares. History and its record in the museums amply testify to the truth of this.

Now all is changed. Traditional art has utterly died out; each man is a freelance, and launches out at manhood into what he has then to learn how to do; and the temptation commonest to most of us is to go into those classes of business which require little apprenticeship and mainly "sharpness," leading more quickly to wealth, than any sort of art or craft. And even in the realms of art itself, there seems an extraordinary desire—fever, may it not be called?—to rush into untrodden paths.

A very large number of youthful designers and artists seem only anxious to design what they call novelty, even at the expense of stamping out tradition entirely—a sort of desire to fly in the face of tradition and get their fame or money simply through the quality of strangeness which they are able to put into their work.

And if, in the practice of more legitimate art or decoration, any man rises out of the commonplace, it is to be accounted for in one of two ways—either that he is a kind of genius, and so naturally out-tops his fellows, or that he possesses, in a high degree, the faculty of assimilating and reproducing the treasures of the past, which, after all, is perhaps only another form of genius.

So that, violent as it may sound, we should, I fear, look with grave doubt and incredulity upon *all* modern productions in fine or decorative art. I do not, of course, say that we should look upon them with scorn or with contempt, but with incredulity, until, after a rigid application of our axioms, we see here and there a form start out from the all but universal slough of degradation into which we have fallen; and then, whether it be a picture by Millais or Burne-Jones, a church of Butterfield's, a house of Norman Shaw's, a stained-glass window by Morris, such names should be held in memory, and their work looked for with anxiety and interest. Considering, however, the scarcity of such men, our daily food in art, in good colour and form, must be sought for at the British Museum, at the National Gallery, at South Kensington, the Louvre, and such-like places.

There is a further reason for this, not so obvious, but possibly even more important.

It seems to have been clearly perceived in the best days of mediaeval art, that the true function of art consists in the embodiment and representation of the ideal—the poetical. It may be an open question whether this was largely a result of the great demand, from ecclesiastics and others, for pictures of religious subjects, or whether it was a mediaeval condition of mind which passed away with the arrival of advanced forms of "progress." But nothing is more certain than that *all* the finest art that has come down to us from Giotto to Raphael (and a great deal that was earlier and later) is ideal in the highest degree, and almost without exception poetical. As to the question of ideality, let us take a single example, as a specimen of the spirit which permeates their art.

No subject is more common, in the finest period of art, than the Nativity, or the Adoration of the Kings. In either case, the infant Christ must have been of extremely tender age; yet nowhere is He represented as a new-born infant—always as a plump, well-developed child of six to twelve months old—an *ideal baby*, in fact in direct disregard of the text of the history it was to illustrate.

The question of poetical treatment as apart—if it can be apart—from ideality, is less easy to exhibit in a moderate compass; but no reflective person can visit the National Gallery, and then the Royal Academy, without perceiving the strong contrast in feeling between the two in style, in frame of mind, in effect on us. It is again not a difference in *degree*, it is a difference in *kind*.

One ranks with Holy Scripture, with Chaucer, with Spenser, with Shakespeare; the other with Darwin, with Herbert Spencer, with the magazines, with the Times. This divergence is exactly the divergence between poetry and prose.

Poetry and mediaeval art come upon us as somewhat strange, somewhat weird and mysterious, rather difficult, requiring all our patience, and often more than all our wits, to comprehend and to assimilate. But once comprehended and taken to heart, they become the constant companions of our better selves; they cherish and amplify our highest aspirations; they lift us up for a while into a finer and purer atmosphere, and, whether we know it or not, they elevate us above the dust and rubbish of our daily lives.

Yet modern realistic art, magazines and newspapers, are friendly and easy, chatty and jocose as boon companions; they appeal instantly to the meanest capacity; make us happy, maybe, as a meal does; make us laugh; help us to pass the time. But they leave us just where we were, in the City or in Bond Street, in the office or the stable.

We have lately heard a good deal about the general improvement in taste which is supposed to have taken place during the last few years. There has been a great deal of change, but has there been any improvement?

To be sure, there are many people of cultivated taste to be found —people who instinctively avoid loud and vulgar things—there always were; though, of course, when "society" was smaller, they were much fewer in number. These people find it now-a-days easier to obtain unobjectionable dress, furniture, and household stuff, than it used to be; and, beyond doubt, a trade of a limited extent has been created by such people, so that they now know where they can find what they want, often ready in stock. But when we consider the enormous increase during the last thirty years in the number of families who can spend £ 600 a year and upwards, it is evident that the trade in moderate and well-designed articles is relatively small and exceptional; and anyone who will take the trouble to go through some of the huge furnishing warehouses in Tottenham Court Road and Finsbury, to go no further, may readily discover that every vile and violent shade that dyers can dye (and they are infinitely viler than they were or could be forty years ago, before the general introduction of aniline), every preposterous form of chair, cabinet, or sofa originated in the most degraded times of George IV, is still completely in vogue with a large proportion of buyers, and is ten times oftener asked for than anything quiet or moderate.

Moreover, everything must now be both low priced and highly ornamented; and among the exigencies so created, there arise terrific visions of all kinds and sizes—lamps, coal-boxes, cheap jewellery, pictures, and chimney-piece ornaments, easy-chairs, curtains—a thousand and one terrors which percolate into our houses. For our friends give them to us, even if we carefully abstain from buying them (who does not know of the young bride who hardly dares to show some of her wedding presents!). They are not only devoid of any one sign of education, or cultivation in their designer, but are manifestly the production of grossly vulgar and illiterate people, and determinedly trample on every canon of decent taste or propriety.

Possibly those who think they can see an improvement are misled, partly by the existence of such a shop as Mr. Morris's, and partly by the recent fashion of wearing quiet and tertiary shades in dress. But this is only a fashion, and if fashion dictates magenta as the colour for dress next year, magenta will be worn triumphantly;[1] while as for the trade in goods of the character of Mr. Morris's productions, it is as a drop in the ocean.

There are two articles usually to be found in the houses of people who can afford to spend twelve hundred a year and more (who may roughly be taken to represent our upper and educated class), a grand piano, and a billiard-table.

They are about the very ugliest things on the earth; and partly from there being only the very feeblest desire to see them improved, and partly from a fear of what Mrs. Grundy will say if they are altered, they have remained a hideous eyesore for fifty years and more. There is absolutely no reason worth the name why both of them should not at least have good mouldings and well-designed legs, and there is every reason why a billiard-table should be lined with a temperate green, restful to the eye, instead of the very crudest and fiercest colour that can be dyed; yet there they stand, two ugly blots in almost every large house in the land. Look again at the houses recently erected and those in course of erection by the speculating builder— say in South Kensington or Chelsea—houses of £ 200 to £ 500 a year rental, and see to what ornament he treats ladies and gentlemen: his cornices, his grates and chimney-pieces, his balusters, his terrible stained glass! But the speculating builder is generally a very clever and acute fellow, feels the pulse of the times, knows "what people like," and gives it, and in consequence he lets his houses in good situations fast, no matter how vile and vulgar be his ornamentations.

When such houses do not let because they are done in bad taste, and ladies and gentlemen have reformed their pianos and billiard-tables, we may begin to believe in the general taste having improved —but not sooner.

Meanwhile, we should try and keep a clean palate. Do not ever be persuaded, however gorgeous the doorway, to visit catch-penny exhibitions of doubtful pictures—no matter whether they be surrounded by maroon velvet or hot-house plants. Avoid all things that are much advertised and puffed, even if the premises be in Bond Street. Never be entrapped into admiring new hotels, even if there be luncheon for nothing; and as for our homes (where we can to some extent regulate our surroundings), we cannot possibly be too exacting or careful to keep out showy rubbish. We should never buy foolish or ignoble photographs on any consideration whatever, and if we have them given to us, we should wait till the donor is out of sight, and then promptly burn them.

When we see vulgar advertisements we should turn our heads the other way; similarly, with representations of French priests grinning, or gobbling oysters, or being shaved (if we all of us avoided buying the soap of people who so offend, we might at least abate that nuisance), or coarse pictures of impossibly fat monks drinking beer, or vulgar caricatures of public men. Photographs from life are also to be avoided, or accepted in homeopathic quantities—a worthless and generally ignoble form of so-called art, which fills up our rooms, unduly engages our attention, and stands to a good many people in the place of art—a vile imposture. If we must have third-rate portraits of our friends, let them be kept in drawers. And let us rid ourselves of all crude and strongly coloured wall-papers, carpets, or curtains-things with feeble and prominent and meaningless designs; emerald green or magenta crochet mats for plants to stand on. *All this supposed-to-be-harmless but conspicuous rubbish, even if it comes from Regent Street, should be consigned to the kitchen fire.* And our axioms, if well and rigidly applied, are quite sufficient to guide us safely to the purchase of fresh curtains, carpets, wall-papers, and chintzes. But perhaps some one will say, "You have burnt or banished most of our pictures and ornamental objects,—how are we to replace them? We can't do without some semblance of fine art on our walls, or bits of good ornament here and there; you destroy, please replace." Without in the least admitting that these axioms would not suffice here also, one cannot deny the reasonableness of the demand; so after this chapter there follows another, giving items of fine art, at prices to meet the exigencies of all pockets, for the walls.

Of course, if we can go to Bond Street dealers, and commission them to buy things which would be welcome at South Kensington Museum, the affair is easy enough; but to buy really good art at prices between twenty shillings and twenty pounds is not so easy, no doubt.

There is another aspect of the matter applying strictly to art students and artists, but eventually, through them, to all of us.

Artists are, in a great measure, our teachers. We learn more quickly through the eye than through the ear; and if we see frivolous and ignoble pictures, we think in those respects frivolously and ignobly. If, on the contrary, the artists take the highest view of their subject, and lead us into a higher atmosphere, we follow them there; so it is of the utmost importance to us as a nation to regulate what frame of mind, what *temper*, what environment the artist shall have in his daily life.

Take what may be supposed to be the popular art of the day, the art one finds in shop windows in Piccadilly and the Strand, and see what sort of subjects people rejoice in. I purposely avoid cultured art lovers, who admire Velasquez, Gainsborough, and Turner, their number being inconsiderable, and the Art they admire is not "popular." Now, it will be found upon examination, that probably half of the popular art exhibited in our shop windows is of a sporting character, if not actually representing horses with jockeys on them, at least horses, dogs, gamekeepers, and that type. A fair proportion may be fancy pictures of the portrait type, mostly women—a good subject, no doubt, but frivolously treated. The rest are largely kittens, puppies, and commonplace scenes of country life, more or less ignoble subjects, rather grossly treated. From Germany we seem to get mainly a feeble sort of religious picture—noble ideas originally, no doubt, but dragged by artists of the level of Overbeck through the mud of a commonplace imagination, till they lose their charm and become no art at all.

If we turn to France, things are still worse. Their art consists so largely in drawings of over-dressed and fast-looking girls, bent on making the best market of their charms, that the remainder do not really seem worth mentioning. Frivolity and sensuality seem to be their lodestars, and their art, such as it is, follows their attraction admirably.

Now turn to the Italian popular art of mediaeval and Renaissance times. The comparison does not go on all fours, because the state of society and its consequent demands, and the appliances for satisfying these demands, did not then exist. But the popular art of that day may undoubtedly be seen at the British Museum, and the print shop where they sell the works of Tintoretto, Titian, and the rest.

The contrast is dispiriting.

Are we to go forward in the race after frivolity and sensuality? It depends much upon artists and architects and the cultured class. If they will be true to the cultivation of real art instead of rubbish, much may be hoped. Unfortunately, as we advance in civilisation, it seems that Romance, the poetic side of us, which is to the human heart what the flower is to the plant, dies out and disappears; and instead of following in the track of our great artists of the past, instead of cultivating in our students the art of dramatic intention, of deep and poetic thought and meaning, romantic situation, suggestive poetry, high aspiration, we go in for teaching them mechanical exactness, endless anatomy, extreme niceties in drawing and detail. This, for our students: for ourselves, cast iron, railways, telegraphs, electric lighting, huge hotels, and—dividends.

Chapter 4
High Art for Shallow Purses

Chromo-lithographs after Turner's Vignettes, at 2s. 6d. each, exceedingly well copied, may be purchased from Messrs. Romney & Co., Oxford Street, London. Four in one frame, with a gold mount, make a reasonably sized and interesting wall ornament.

Photographs of the Terra-Cottas of Lucca della Robbia, and other similar decorative Italian work, are sold by G. Cole, Via Tornabuoni, Florence, at two to three francs each.

The Chromo-lithographs published by the Arundel Society, after mediaeval Italian art, are many of them excellent and interesting. It is not necessary to be a subscriber in order to obtain them, and an old subscriber, whether he has ceased to subscribe or not, may always obtain them for himself or his friends at subscriber's prices. Office in St. James's Street, London.

Turner's "Liber Studiorum" prints in sepia (a great part of the work by the artist himself). At a Bond Street shop ten guineas and upwards is asked, but I have bought many at the small, insignificant shops lying between the Strand and Oxford Street, at one and a half to four guineas.

Small Eighteenth Century Engravings, mostly printed in brown, and generally circular or oval in shape, after Angelica Kauffman, Cipriani, and others; imaginative and poetical subjects, illustrating Spenser's "Faery Queen," &c. Sold by old print collectors in Soho, &c. (must be bought with care, there being plenty of rubbishy imitations). Some of the best are printed on cream-coloured satin.

F. Hollyer, Pembroke Square, Earl's Court Road, Kensington, prints and sells a very fine collection of most interesting photographs, after Burne-Jones and D. G. Rossetti. These photographs are quite of a superior style to the ordinary article.

Bartolozzi's Engravings, after Holbein, some of them on tinted paper, may often be met with in old book and print shops in London, at 5s. to 10s., and the three or four best of them at £ 2, 2s. or £ 3, 3s. They were published by Chamberlain in A.D. 1793, and the whole book (which contains at least twenty-five worth framing) may occasionally be met with at prices varying from 25 to 35 guineas, according to the condition of the plates. They are most excellent and interesting.

Albert Durer's Woodcuts, reproduced of late years in France, very vigorous and picturesque, at a few francs; and for those who have patience to hunt further, original woodcuts and etchings by Durer and his best imitators are often to be picked up at small prices, 10s. and upwards, especially if rather foxed, or if they have lost their margins.

Mezzotint Engravings, published about 1790, many of them in a beautiful deep soft brown, after Gainsborough, Reynolds, Romney, and Hoppner, may often be found at old print shops at £ 5, 5s. and upwards, according to condition. They are printed on exceedingly soft paper, and so are often out of condition, and proportionately cheap. They are easy to mount when wetted thoroughly all over, and may then be touched up with a very fine sable and Indian ink. Nothing has of late years been so much looked up by lovers of art, and fine proof copies have frequently been sold at upwards of 100 guineas each by auction. The most beautiful are generally full-length portraits of ladies.

Copies of the most valuable and interesting works in the National Gallery, or of parts of them, may be purchased during the process of copying, at such prices as ten to thirty guineas. There are "hacks," no doubt, who produce bad copies all through a lifetime, but there are also many excellent copyists, who like the work, and are glad of the little pocket-money so earned; and to sensible people, who don't want to brag of the value of their possessions, such copies are quite as interesting as the originals.

Of course, it is not pretended that this is a complete list of all the objects of high art that may be obtained at such prices.

ORNAMENT

I need not say that much pleasure, much cultivation of taste, and great improvement to the aspect of the house may be obtained by buying for chimney-piece and cabinet ornaments, in place of the trash annually poured out by Birmingham and the Potteries, Paris and Munich, such things as the following:

Old Blue and White Oriental China.—Good vases and beakers are costly, but plates are often as good in design, and remain moderate in price.

Rhodian Ware, often called Persian, generally plates. Greyish-cream ground, with variously coloured flowers. Very conventional.

Modern Venetian Glass.—The simpler and more severely shaped pieces, generally in the form of tall wine-glasses and beakers.

Modern Lustre Ware.—Dishes by Cantagalli, of Florence, and by De Morgan of Great Marlborough Street, London.

Old Brass Dishes.—By no means very rare. Are still in use in Italy in the fried-fish shops.

Scraps of Old Embroidery, Italian or English. These may be arranged as panels in an over-mantel, or for screens.

"Chippendale" Mirrors, so called, though never figured by Chippendale. Small, mahogany-framed, usually with a carved and gilt bird at the top, and pierced thin woodwork above and below. Also broad, black Venetian mirror-frames (*cornice a sbalzo*), with little waved patterns on their mouldings.

Old Flemish Leather, stamped and lacquered, making an excellent frieze or backing to a sideboard.

Old French or Flemish Tapestry, of the kind known as "Verdure"—trees, shrubs, and landscape only. Unimportant pieces, of moderate dimensions, often change hands at 40s. per square yard.

And by the use of Oriental carpets, rugs, and mattings, wherever practicable, in lieu of those of English manufacture. (It is quite possible, however, to buy very bad ones—the "axioms" should be kept well in mind.)

Chapter 5
Decoration of the House

Before dealing with a subject which must of necessity consist largely of almost querulous fault-finding, I wish to say, quite plainly and distinctly, how highly I hold in esteem the calling of an architect— not merely regarded as an ideal of what an architect may and ought to be—but practically, as I have found architects I have known, and under whom I have worked for years, and from a knowledge of what they have done and what they are doing.[2] The most beautiful and enduring things the world possesses we owe to their education and their patience, their ingenuity and love; and if a man wants to be transformed and elevated—the beast in him to be subdued and the God-like developed—let him trace the history of architecture and visit her creations, from the Parthenon and the French and English cathedrals to the Houses of Parliament, and your own St. George's Hall (Liverpool).

If I have any fault to find with architects, it is that they do not go far enough; that they should not stop their activity at wall and cornice and woodwork, but that they should also design the ceiling, the frieze, the dado, the chimney-piece, the grate, the electric fittings, and not leave all these things to dribble into the hands of a set of uneducated shopkeepers, whose only interest is £ s. d.

In an age of low and sordid ambitions, when every man is greedy to rob his neighbour if he can, it seems a matter of inestimable value to the public weal that there should exist a body of men who are, for the most part, educated gentlemen; who are seldom commercially ambitious; who can take delight in beauty of form and colour for beauty's sake, and *not* because it *pays*; who are singularly tenacious of each other's rights, rather than of their own; whose value to the community is never adequately acknowledged; who constantly do as good or better work than the painters, but who are not one-tenth part so much flattered and petted; and who habitually work hard for their living, and very seldom have the chance of a plum.

It is to these qualities we must look for our bulwarks against the tide of vulgar, commonplace, and utilitarian rubbish, which threatens at present to absorb every calling. The world seems to have entered upon a new phase, distinguished principally by a desire to make money, irrespective of the way it is made; and we are following our American neighbours across the Atlantic in falling down to worship the Almighty Dollar. There is no apparent breakwater to stem the tide but that of architects and artists, if they will, who have, something to set up as a goal better worth winning than commercial success.

Decoration.—No one will surely attempt to deny that we live in an age conspicuous for its commonplace. Whether it be the average builder's house, or civil engineer's railway station, or a scientific man's electric fittings, we recognise modern work by its complete absence of character. Now, commonplace is dull and uninteresting. No one would knowingly seek it or desire it, or, unless he were desperately dull and commonplace himself, would pay good money to get it; and yet most people *do* get it. They rent or buy commonplace houses with commonplace decoration, and complete the thing with commonplace furniture; and it becomes an inquiry of some interest to try and see how this arises, and what are the chief inducing causes. A decorator becomes so wearied and worried by the mountains of commonplace stuff around, that the subject has become an interesting study, and we seem to trace its origin in a sort of misdirected utilitarianism. Now, that brings us upon tangible ground.

As an example: I suppose I am only one among many who have been rash enough to attempt to improve the mouldings and details of a billiard-table and a piano, but always with this result, that it has been proved to me by the foreman or masters of such an establishment, that in several cases the new details supplied would have cost a little more money. This one cut into more wood; another wanted cutting at twice; in a third they had been accustomed to cut two out of a square, and the new drawing was not so accommodating—and so on through the list.

Now, this spirit is to be found in every branch of trade, and in ninety-nine cases out of a hundred it is just the little interesting and artistic touch that is found to be more costly or less convenient. Something must be pinched to meet the competition. Wages cannot be altered; material and labour must, therefore, be economised. A cabriole leg to a chair requires a carver: a turned leg can be done by the thousand in a steam lathe. A large design goes over three or four printing-blocks: cut it down in dimensions and put it in on one. A sheep-skin for embossing costs 3s. 6d., but paper as stout can be had for 4½ d. A door handle with a ray-like set of flutings must be cast and chased leave out the flutings, and you can "spin" it. And so in every department of work, except, perhaps, those details of a building upon which a good architect rests his reputation, we drop down to utilitarian commonplace.

And the motive force which brings this about is that terrible commercial desire to do the largest business possible, rather than to be content to do a smaller business, and to do it as well as it possibly can be done.

Your spirited and enterprising tradesman, with the mercantile instinct very strongly developed, advertises freely and lies freely, and assures all who will read or listen to him that they can live as well, own as pretty houses, and dress as well, as far as appearances go, as their richer neighbours. His competitors of the same street advertise and lie even more freely than he does; and down goes the price of every commodity, the *value* going down still more quickly— for, are not the savings all made out of material? And as if this was not bad enough, it seems that, to spice the dish, it is necessary to offer the bait of continual novelty—novelty in the spring, further novelty in the autumn; and to produce this, huge establishments are required, divided into sections, over each of which presides a manager, trained only in the art of dividend-making; the whole being quite beyond the reach of the taste, or influence, or even of the personal scrutiny of the real master—utilitarianism being the only god they all worship.

You will ask, perhaps, how this is to be stopped. That, I fear, would lead us beyond the limits of an inquiry like this; but at least we may each do much by fostering the opposite spirit, by carefully avoiding tradesmen who are prominent advertisers, and by influencing our families and friends to do so too.

In comparing, to our constant chagrin and vexation, the beautiful productions of the Middle Ages—tapestry, leather, armour, pottery, figured velvets, embroidery, and the like, with the cheap rubbish of today, one cannot but ask how it was that they, with fewer facilities than we, produced this wealth and abundance of beautiful things, while we, with all the results of their experience to help us, seem comparatively impotent. I confidently ascribe it to the loss of tradition—that whereas the mediaeval armourer was generally the son and grandson of an armourer, and brought up his son and his grandson to be armourers too, the painter was the son and possibly the grandson of a painter, the tapestry-weaver also being descended from a family of tapestry-makers and so on through every trade, the country being filled with young men who from boyhood understood their business, and had no thought but of practising the same. Nowadays, we go off into the opposite direction, and our successful upholsterer is the son of a city clerk, and brings up *his* son to be a country gentleman and a breeder of race-horses.

William Morris used to say that the sixteenth century craftsman lived so happily and joyously, was so well dressed, and housed, and fed (his master being jovial and liberal too), that out of the sheer delight he found in his life and surroundings, he thought beautiful things, hammered beautiful iron, embossed beautiful leather, wove beautiful tapestry, and sang jovial songs. I hope it is all true.

But I think it has been proved beyond dispute that the workman was never nearly so well off in the history of the world as he is today. An examination of old workmen's quarters that still exist in France and Italy, the Rue de Jerzuel in Dinan, for instance, which have scarcely been touched for two or three hundred years, and the dark and narrow *calles* of Venice, and slum areas in Paris and Rome, seem to show that the mediaeval workman was very badly housed in what we should call dark and dirty quarters. No doubt such details are matters of comparison, and probably their quarters were as good as they desired, their needs not having been increased by the sight of anything better—for their class, at least. The workman gained, of course, immensely by the comparative smallness of the towns and thinness of the population as compared with our own. The power of joining in the field sports of the nobles, if only as lookers-on, must have been a great relief, and even, with some natures, it is conceivable that war might have been an agreeable change. Hours of work, we can well understand, must have been less arbitrary, and more according to the workman's own choice; and the power of carrying on his work at his own house must have been an enormous gain when we think of the crowded factory of the present day; so that his life, when compared with that of today, may have been tolerable.

In each age, no doubt, the ruling class gets what it wants and has the money to pay for. In the sixteenth century, money was but in the hands of the few. The mediaeval prince, or baron, or squire, the bishop or canon of the Church, knew how to rule the roost, and, in a rough way, they did it well; and these beautiful things we are talking about were what they liked and wanted, and had the money to pay for; and it was just that traditional craftsmanship we have spoken about which rendered it, in difficult and troublesome times, still possible for certain trades to live—though, judging by history, the workmen could not have worked more than half their time—war filling up the other half.

Yet, how different are the social conditions now. Where there were one or two of the ruling class in a town or neighbourhood, there are now a thousand burghers, all fairly well-to-do, whose wants are of an entirely different kind. They desire and enjoy better houses, more warmth and protection from cold, gas, improved lamps, electric light, better and more varied food, books, magazines, newspapers, and postal services—a much better *ménage*, extending, too, all over the house; music, and occasionally foreign travel; while the richer ones desire and obtain costlier equipage, good art, a great deal too much sport, and two or three houses each, instead of one, not to mention long sojourns in foreign hotels.

Collectively, this modern society demands, and gets, good means of transport by land and by sea, rapid transmission of messages or news, and comfortable hotels at all centres of interest, whether in the streets of a metropolis or on a Swiss mountain. These are the demands of the burgher of the latter half of the present century—for a great many of us no longer desire to lord it, baronially, with fire and sword, but are learning to live and let live; and a vast section of society now prefers to live honourably by the sweat of the brow, rather than screw rack-rents out of pauper peasants. The pluck, ingenuity, and industry of the designing and working class of our time has produced the article demanded, and has been liberally paid for it. True, the details of the articles so produced are in most cases as hideous as utilitarianism can make them; but remember that it was not beautiful detail that was ordered, but material comfort and convenience; and, beyond doubt, if beautiful leather for wall coverings, for instance, had been steadily asked for twenty years ago, some of us would have produced leather equal to the best the Spaniards made, and by now better still. But the well-to-do burgher replies, "I do not care to pay a guinea a skin: I would rather have an imitation at 5s., and spend the remainder in dogs, horses, yachts, Scotch shooting, a trip to the Riviera." We may be sorry for his choice and think it a mistake, but we have to deal with facts, and change our ideas with the changing times.

Perhaps you will say to me, "Well, but if the production of beautiful sixteenth century work were to be demanded again, say by an aristocracy who had ceased to think killing God's creatures the greatest pleasure to be enjoyed, you would merely copy old work: you would go to South Kensington and trace and copy and reproduce." Believe me, this has always been so. No architect, no painter, no craftsman in this world ever sprung by a stride into what was at once novel and good.

And just as the beautiful Gothic of Beauvais and Bourges is merely developed through a thousand delicate gradations from a Greek temple, *so whatever work of man's is thoroughly fine and noble in the world, must always have been only a trifling advance upon a previous success.* There is absolutely no exception whatever to this rule.

The more one looks into the history of the past, the more one feels that each art or craft must follow its own tradition. I know we live in an age when this is constantly forgotten, and numbers of young designers and architects are constantly springing up to show how they can make mighty leaps and astonish the ages. There were three or four specimens in a recent "Arts and Crafts Exhibition," where the modern gesso work was cracked and going to pieces within a few months of its production. The saving clause is that these crazes are of short duration; and we are constantly learning that tradition is the only safe foundation.

In the first half of the last century the increasing wealth of the nation, the constant visits to France and Belgium of soldiers and statesmen, and the ideas so communicated to men at home, brought about a great ferment amongst the well-to-do classes as regards the houses they lived in and their fittings, and made us very conscious that our manner of living was barbarous in comparison with that of our Continental neighbours.

Where a genuine demand exists, there seem always the men produced to supply it, and Robert and John Adam, who published their magnificent work in 1773, appear to have drawn in careful detail, not only the houses they built, but all the furniture for them, including even the draping of the curtains. Witness the superb collection of their drawings now to be seen at the Soane Museum. And other architects of that time, if they do not go quite so far as the Adams, at all events published excellent books of engravings, often with full-sized details, of chimney-pieces and ceilings, which are not only the best for our modern wants that have ever been designed, but continue to form the best models for our work of today. George Richardson, who published his work in 1776, stands, perhaps, in the van (for the Adams' work was exceptional, and for the very rich).

The Chimney-piece.—The chimney-piece is a great feature in determining the character of a room, and though I cannot think of placing these men in front of the great Renaissance designers of Italy, yet for the average burgher's house, the designs of W. Jones, Inigo Jones, N. Wallis, and Matthias Darley, besides the two already mentioned, form a most valuable heirloom.

But the whole series of illustrated books, commencing with W. Jones in 1739, and terminating with Sheraton at the end of the century, forms a most wonderful chapter in the history of English architecture and decoration. It embraced, besides the architects mentioned, and several not mentioned, Chippendale, Shearer, Heppelwhite, and Sheraton, cabinetmakers; Lock, Copeland, and Johnson, wood carvers; the delightful Pergolesi, Cipriani, and Columbani, designers of ornament; and many others of more or less merit. And though there was a dangerous disposition to be wild and flamboyant, and even to try and out-Frank the French, yet underneath it all there is a solid residuum of good grain well worth the necessary sifting. The architects, of course, followed Greece and Rome. The cabinetmakers and carvers drew their inspiration beyond doubt from France (buying the illustrated books of Berain, Le Pautre, and others). The ornamenters were Italians pure and simple, imported adults. Nevertheless, it was these men, apparently, that rescued us from a state of rude barbarism in all these arts, and they were on the highroad to place us abreast of our neighbours, when the French Revolution, at one blow, cut us off from most of the sources of our inspiration, and we dropped at once to commonplace and humdrum. Anyone who will take the trouble to wade through the shelves of illustrated books at South Kensington cannot but be struck by the astonishingly rapid collapse of all that was valuable or useful in those published after Sheraton. Up to his time (1791), every book contained something of merit, but even his own latest book (1804), Taylor (1804), Wood (1806), G. Smith (1808), are tissues of impotent vulgarity, and form the origin of all that bad work of the early part of the century which makes one alternately laugh and shudder.

And just as the Chippendale period, 1740 to 1795, has left us a fine legacy, in chimney-pieces, ceilings, furniture and decoration, so the dull and humdrum period, 1800 to 1850, has left us a dreadful residuum of hideous ceiling rosettes, huge and imbecile cornices, generally with a large cavetto; white marble chimney-pieces with an arch and trusses, large mirrors, always with a half-oval head, and cut glass chandeliers. And these again (it is like the sowing of dragon's teeth) have produced the immense skirting, vulgar mouldings everywhere; the terrible gasalier; the builder's "sham," carrying bad tiles fixed in a frame; cornices, still huger and more full of frivolous and foolish enrichments; the window with only two panes of glass, and other enormities. We must all do our best utterly to forget and ignore the terrible period between 1793 and 1870—the seventy-seven years following the French Revolution.

The Ceiling.—We have been for long, and still are, though there are signs of improvement, quite stupid as regards the ceiling. No doubt, ever since good Queen Bess's time at least, architects have generally contrived to put one moulded plaster ceiling, if not more, into the houses of the rich—but there things have stopped until quite lately; and the average citizen's ceilings consist of from thirty to sixty square yards of plain, whitewashed plaster.

We decorate our walls with patterns and pictures and cabinets and mirrors, and then pretend that we "rather prefer a plain ceiling."

The modelled ceiling of the last century, if it gained in refinement on the Stuart work, lost heavily in want of breadth and mass, and was constantly spotty and liny. But the illustrated works of Matthias Darley, Robert and John Adam, and Richardson, to go no further, afford some charming ideas of ceiling arrangements, and when executed mainly in colour, they must have been most lovely, and are fine examples for our use.

Not enough use is made of flock paper. Ten or twelve flocks give a much bolder relief than "Anaglypta," and nearly as much relief as the well-known "Tynecastle," and cost less. But it is to be hoped that as architects come to design more and more of the interior fittings of their houses, they will give sketches in colour for the ceilings, and call on us decorators to carry them out. For, with our cloudy skies, it is *colour* above all things that we want in our houses. There is no reason why our ceilings should not be as well and carefully coloured as our walls, if only huge cornices and dreadful rosettes could be kept out of them. No doubt, the ceiling wants more delicate colouring than the wall—a piece of experience that quickly comes to any designer; but to lay down a rule that nothing but a white ceiling is admissible is about as sensible as to say that nothing but a green wall is admissible. Rooms should be coloured in accordance with their aspect; and no relief, however interesting, can be so beautiful for a room to be used at night, as a painted and delicately coloured ceiling.

There is plenty of paper painted in watercolour, by artists of the sixteenth century, in good condition now; and a paper ceiling with printed borders and hand-painted foliages and plaques can be executed at half the cost of a Tynecastle or moulded ceiling, and comes within the price that the average house-building John Bull can pay. Pergolesi alone, brought to this country by the Adams, has left us in his book a perfect mine of wealth as to the treatment of ceilings.

The Cornice.—There is no more mischievous feature than the huge cornice which the builder always puts into his house. He thinks, I suppose, to make his room look "handsome." Never, under any circumstances, can it be otherwise than an eyesore. The cornice should be large enough to take the eye off the bareness of a right angle, and no larger. Almost every old house in London (at least of a hundred years old) shows us specimens of beautiful cornices of not more than eight or nine inches in girth, even less. The decoration of the ceiling and the wall is much facilitated by this, and such a cornice, if painted a subdued white, retires, as it should, into its proper place, and tempts nobody to the dreadful process of picking out; a tiny leaf or scroll in the lower part, and a bold, square member in the middle, finished by a simple moulding above and below, being all that is wanted. It is wonderful how well one can manage to do without cornices altogether in the less important rooms, if some modest sum be allowed for paper borders. Indeed, if everything is to cost nearly nothing, as seems the fashion nowadays, why not give up the bedroom cornice at once; and even in reception rooms, where the builder, for some cause or other, has omitted the cornice, it will be found that a wooden moulding of two or three inches in girth looks well.

The Frieze.—The frieze is to the constructional part of the room what the flower or fruit is to the plant, and can scarcely receive too much careful attention.

Being well above the line where pictures and ornaments and cabinets come, a dull region remains there if you have no frieze; and the absence of one nearly always results in the undue enlargement of the cornice, which gets filled with "enrichments," and becomes a slough of despond. The frieze is too often entirely forgotten, or left to the imagination of the local decorator. Architects ought always to provide one, except in the exceedingly low rooms of a cottage; and there are so many ways of treating this most ornamental feature. Let me enumerate:

(a.) There is cast plaster ornament, of which (even if you have a mould to make) the cost is reasonable.

(b.) For those who want something original, a young artist can paint on gilded canvas, and give the room a character which nothing else will give so well.

(c.) Stencilled paper also makes a charming frieze, with delicacies of colour and design which I think no other plan can equal.

(d.) For the least important rooms there are printed friezes which, carefully chosen, may be adequate and agreeable.

But an architect who has any originality should take this opportunity of giving distinguishing character to his room, by a picturesque and original frieze of his own design; and the owner of the house, or his wife, if they can paint, should paint their own.

The Body of the Wall.—The great advantage of large designs is evident, but a very great deal too much fuss is made about wall papers. People seem to think that if they have bought a Morris wall paper, that they have gone three-fourths of the way to a beautifully decorated room; whereas it is quite possible that a plain, or nearly plain wall, with a dado and frieze more or less ornamental, might have been far better than any sort of pattern. Our rooms often get terribly over-patterned—patterned wall and ceiling, patterned floor, patterned curtains, patterned furniture-covers; where are we to get a little rest for the eye, if not occasionally by a plain wall? But supposing that, for sufficient reasons, the wall is to be patterned, the design should be the largest possible. I am not at all forgetting the charm and constant advantage of diaper patterns, sometimes even on a minute scale; but I am now speaking of the large wall spaces between the dado and the frieze, which roughly may be considered as spaces of ten square yards and upwards on the average.

Of course, the "local" decorator is sure to recommend "a neat small pattern," partly because small, characterless patterns are cheap, easy, and safe, and involve no responsibility, and partly because the constant desire for novelty (new patterns each spring, and more new patterns each autumn) almost necessitate the adoption of small designs on the part of the printer, in order to be reasonably economical in the expense of block-cutting. Here again utilitarianism steps in. We may not have an old pattern, because it is old, and novelty is necessary. ("Let us be in the fashion or die.") And we cannot have large patterns, because the blocks would be costly. Out with such nonsense! Let us have adequate, fine designs, even if we have to stick to them for twenty years.

Anyone who has given attention to the beautiful designs often to be found on the dresses and draperies in fine old paintings, must have noticed that in nine cases out of ten the painter never allows a "repeat" to appear. Damask designs behind a Blessed Virgin, or on her dress, are always large patterns with no repeat shown, the repeat being manifestly understood to be the weak point of the ornament, and likely to be tiresome and limiting. Yet Mr. Voysey has discovered in this *fin de siècle* that this is not so, and even draws patterns in express contradiction of this theory, of which more later on.

Any of us having a wall to decorate, say about 10 feet x 10 feet, and expense being no great object, would at once feel that the ideal way would be to commence the pattern with some root or basal feature on the skirting, and finish with lighter and finial features against the frieze or cornice, filling the space right and left with a pleasantly varied arrangement of harmonious forms. We should never bother ourselves with a repeat, except on utilitarian grounds. When you come to bring this into practical working, the cost of a huge set of blocks becomes at once a prohibition, for even a set of blocks 8 feet x 21 inches is somewhat of a difficulty to the printer.

But there is a way—and an old way too—of getting over the difficulty—namely, by stencilling. There is no practical difficulty about making stencil plates in varnished cartridge-paper the height of the wall you have to decorate, and the expense is not unreasonable. Moreover, stencilling produces much finer colouring than printing, and gives the effect of handwork, as indeed it mainly is, taking at once a higher position than the much more mechanical block-printing.

Stencilling is one of the most beautiful of decorative arts. The stencil-plate, costing little, can be thrown aside, when one room has been decorated, without undue expense, thereby getting rid of the terrible mechanical appearance of our rooms, which become exactly like other people's rooms, or remind us of them. The accomplished stenciller finds no bounds to the gradation of colouring which he can produce—gradation, not only between flower and flower, thereby entirely hiding the repeat; but, if he pleases, gradation between the lower part next the skirting and the higher part next the cornice.

It is a class of work that has been relegated to mean little borders and mechanical detail in churches, and so used, it generally produces a very bad effect. But it is capable of all sorts of beautiful variations, and should at once regain its proper position in these crafts. On the mere question of gradation alone, it is worthy of the highest consideration, for, as Mr. Ruskin has well said, "Colour begins where gradation begins."

There is a supposition amongst a large number of people that a small room requires a small pattern on the wall. This is a distinct mistake. There is no sort of relation between the size of the room and the size of the wall pattern. The smallest of boudoirs will bear the largest of designs, if the pattern be only not aggressive. The real relation between these things is between the size of the room and the energy or force of the design; a little room requiring a modest arrangement of chiaroscuro and colour, while a large hall or ballroom may be best treated with a pattern full of force and light and shade, and telling colouring.

It may be well at this point to consider the much belauded Japanese ornament. It is a little difficult to discuss it with patience and reasonableness: its perfervid admirers are so unreasonable in their frantic adulation. Ordinarily, in Europe at all events, we do not say of any man that he can draw until he has accurately delineated things which of their nature demand complete exactness, such as the human form, or a fine cathedral interior, with arcades and vaultings in many planes. Now a Japanese artist never, under any circumstances, draws such things as these, and from what one sees of his work, one may say with confidence that he is unable to do so. If his work, therefore, be art, it is art under exceedingly narrow limitations, and cannot be thought of as high art at all. When "artists" cannot "draw," one wants to know what they are there for. We all know that a man may go on copying leaves and flowers for fifty years, and yet be unable to "draw" the hand that drew them; and we call him a designer or a decorator, not an artist. You may search in vain from the time that Sir Rutherford Alcock first brought Japanese work to this country, and never find a Japanese design which could be called well-balanced, and which readily arrived at a good "repeat," as an Italian's almost always does.

Someone has said that one quality of art is that it should elicit surprise in the beholder; and we must certainly grant the existence of this very minor quality in much of their work. But viewed in due relation to Greek art, or sixteenth century Renaissance art, or the work of Botticelli, Durer, Van Eyck, Rembrandt, Millais, and Burne-Jones, Japanese work can have no definite position whatever, and must be marked "nowhere"; and no one who has any wide and well-considered views on art and artists could ever make the mistake of extolling it as art. The strange furore which has raged around it these last twelve years has arisen from a certain movement or development among ourselves, and not from any merit existing in the Japanese work.

As facilities for intercourse and reading have multiplied, and hand-books on decoration and furnishing have been printed by the score, a great awakening has ensued, principally among women, with regard to our home surroundings, and an excitement and thirst for novelty, *if it can be had cheap*, has raged like a pestilence, Japanese fans, col-oured prints, umbrellas, toys, china, knick-knacks, &c. ("all this lot for 9d."), here come in and appeal to a number of people, who sud-denly discover that they are born decorators, and go utterly crazy about it, and insist that it is a living art—"the only living art," &c.—and the press, only too glad of something fresh at any cost, echoes the cry; till a well-known Regent Street establishment, some half-dozen years ago, had already furnished some two hundred and fifty "Japa-nese rooms" in London alone.

A protest, too, should be made against Englishmen's rooms being "fitted up" as Turkish divans, which are just as false and foolish under the altered circumstances as the two hundred and fifty Japanese rooms. Why cannot we enjoy a queer, strange sixpenny fan, or a blue china jar from the East, and possess it in peace and in due relation to other pretty and beautiful things, without wanting to see the room made to match, which it can never possibly do? It is right enough that the South Kensington Museum should show us a Turkish divan as a historic curiosity, with possible traces of old Persian art in it; but to carry the fashion into our houses is preposterous and idiotic.

Among our modern "cranks," we have a number of designers who think it is necessary to be strange in order to be successful. Con-sciously or unconsciously, these men say to each other, "Go to, let us be queer," whether because their idiosyncrasies lead them that way, or because they think that commercial success is best attained by cultivating notoriety.

It is amazing to see designs drawn, apparently in sober earnest, of which the main intention is the insistence laid on mere lateral repeat, which of all things one would have expected a designer to conceal. Another gives a terrible travesty of humanity—women that make you shudder, men that give you a nightmare. A third draws landscapes of which you do not know the meaning until you are informed. It is not possible that many of these designs can be drawn with any other intention than that of astonishing the spectator; though what comfort or advantage or gain there can be in that process it is difficult to understand.

If it were possible to say or do anything which would conclusively prove that the only safe foundation of design is *tradition*, these abortions would seem to hit the mark, and be a warning to younger men to avoid such quicksands.

We naturally and properly place the Italians far before all other nations as designers of ornament. Lovely work comes to us from old Spain and the Low Countries; and Germany and France have also contributed to our store; but it will be found upon examination that all the best of these productions have an Italian origin. In the early centuries the Italians were wonderfully in touch with Greece, bringing over Greeks to work for them; and with such a beginning, who can wonder that, surrounded on all sides by men who could "draw," the Italian craftsman should have risen as he did by the fifteenth century to the top of the ladder, freely distancing all competitors, and leaving us a treasure-house of design which may well be called inexhaustible? One hears much from the literary art-seekers on the wonders of Persian art, and no doubt the art of the East, such as it is, or was, has a Persian origin; but no Persian designer can for one moment stand beside men of the calibre of Botticelli and Michael Angelo.

The Dado.—The Dado clearly has its use. It represents, as Mr. Ruskin has pointed out, the plinth or base of the wall; it keeps furniture from damaging the decorations, and it enables one to have a plain and delicate tone above, which may stop before you descend to those parts where traffic would soon spoil it.

An imitation panelling, formed by moulded laths, glued and bradded on, has manifest advantages; the whole surface being painted a uniform tone, along with the woodwork of the room.

The more picturesque classes of India matting make an excellent dado covering for passages and other places where the traffic of the house deals hardly with the lower part of the wall, or where people want to lean against the wall, as in a billiard-room.

Besides this, flock paper, going even to the extent of ten flocks in thickness, forms a surface when sized and varnished, or sized and painted, almost as hard and enduring as wood. And possibly the poker work, much in vogue among young ladies, might be utilised here in diaper patterns. And worsted velvet, hung loose in little folds, gives a remarkable sense of finish and cosiness.

The Floor.—With the old-fashioned nine-inch simple skirting, which is far the best, the very plainest of patterns should be chosen for the floor, if parquetry is to be used. Good as is the plain herringbone all in one wood, three-inch boards, like the deck of a ship, are better still.

As to deal floors, the stain and varnish plan is thoroughly unsatisfactory, the thresholds becoming quite shabby in six months. Deal floors should be entirely covered up, either with India matting or felt (the worst of felt being that it often wears badly and fades quickly). One cannot use that useful but ugly linoleum in the bulk of rooms, though it may serve occasionally for the surrounding of a dining-room. Perhaps, on the whole, a nearly plain Brussels carpet is the best, with an Axminster or Oriental carpet in the centre.

The inconvenience of the old Oriental carpet for our modern life is that it is always of the wrong shape—that is, never square, or nearly square, always long and narrow; while the modern Oriental carpet is generally hideous, and frequently not good in material. The patent

Axminster carpet comes, however, to the rescue, for it forms an admirable medium for obtaining an exact copy of the old Persian, with all its rather queer irregularities and freaks of colouring, and is, moreover, a most excellent and useful fabric.

Painting.—The average painter's work, even when smooth and mechanically good (country work is generally the reverse), is unsatisfactory in the extreme. Except white, and the very darkest shades of all, paint is open to the accusation of being fat, clayey, and chalky, and, under the condition known to painters as "flat," friable, and useless. And there is no doubt that the old grained oak, of which we are all sick, on account of its wriggles and affectations and knots, was better, and far more enduring work. The curious thing is that, when we began to see the folly of the affected imitation of the rays and knots of wood, no one seems to have thought of telling the grainer to use his comb alone, and to use it straight, retaining the useful work and getting rid of the folly. At worst it was transparent work, and the fat and clayey aspect was not there. Practically there is not the shadow of a reason why we should not have all colours, even ivory white, painted transparent, and with very great aesthetic advantage all round; the colours are much more beautiful, less positive, less mechanical. There is no difficulty but the temporary one of the lack of painters who will consent to do it, for no doubt it involves a little more care, and in the quirks and angles of mouldings much more care.

Flatting should be positively forbidden. A housemaid can wash it off, as if it were water colour.

Staining.—The staining of wood must not be forgotten. All the light-coloured woods, even oak, if they are good in quality, can be stained quite advantageously; but so much depends on the grain, its regularity and evenness of absorption (varying from one log to another), that it is necessary to watch carefully how the wood behaves under the application of the stain, before you can instruct the workmen what to do. The best colouring matters to use are also the most transparent, such as Prussian blue, deep yellow madder, burnt sienna, Vandyke brown, ground in oil or spirit as the workman may prefer; but it is a process in which the amateur is more likely to succeed than the professional painter.

Effect of Colour.—As regards the general effect of the colouring of a house, the greatest difficulty is in the use of blue. No room, no matter what aspect it has, should ever have the whole of its walls painted or papered blue; and yet many blues are so attractive, and make so good a background for pictures, that there will be always people who prefer it. A safe way is to take care that the cornice and ceiling are white, and the frieze mainly white, that the dado and woodwork are quite white, and then the remainder of the wall may be safely blue.

Green, having many more elements of variety in it, and admitting of a copious admixture of yellow, is safer; but immoderately used, it is very apt to make a house sad-looking; and that, above all things, in this climate, is to be dreaded.

Reds are good, exactly in proportion as they contain an ample supply of yellow, getting thereby a quality which readily illumines under artificial light. The old crimson wall-paper of fifty years ago lighted up no better than a green or blue. Burnt sienna, stippled or, glazed transparent on white, is the most beautiful red in the world.

Yellow, however, is the useful colour for the decorator. It represents sunshine to the mind; and we are creatures of emotion. It is a colour at once beautiful, safe, and satisfactory; capable of more gradation and variety than any other, and nearly impossible to go wrong in, if once you get your workman off the use of chromes, or allow them only in infinitesimal doses. There is one yellow-raw sienna which of itself is capable of more beautiful gradations than any other pigment, if painters and printers would only use it alone.

The ordinary manner of mixing colours in a body of white lead is the worst that can be imagined, and in easel work is well known to be productive of all mischief. The white should be laid on first, so as to get a permanent body of lead, and the colours—or stainings, as they are well called—should be glazed or stippled upon it, one at a time, afterwards. But many good pigments are constantly ruined by being carelessly and cheaply prepared, and good work should always be done with tube colour.

A difficult question, and one often asked, is this: Why such and such a colour (mauve, for instance) is a bad or useless colour for decoration. And here is a suggestion for consideration, viz., that colours are good, safe, and available in proportion as they bear the admixture of yellow: just as sunshine illumines, and thereby yellows the fields and woods. Now, mauve and the purples disappear and become grey when yellow is added, and emerald-green and Prussian-blue alter their character entirely, and become reasonable colours. It will be found that this is a good, safe, all-round test.

Blinds.—Surely never was anything uglier brought into our houses than the ordinary roller-blinds. Whether they are up or down, they are entirely hideous, even with cheap lace at the lower edge. They are particularly apt to go wrong, either in the way they roll up, or in their cords or other tackle. The last lap dirties far sooner than the rest, and, as they come down from above, they inevitably exclude the best light that comes into the room, when they are pulled down. No doubt they have been adhered to as being rather less cumbersome, and because their cords hurt the fingers less, than the terrible Venetian-blind; but in a well-furnished house they are today inexcusable.

I hope to live long enough to see roller-blinds entirely done away with, or relegated only to the kitchen and office. A little curtain, pulling right and left on a small rod close to the glass, answers the purpose better, and is agreeable and picturesque where the roller is hideous. The best material for sitting-rooms is the natural silk of the East—tussore or shantung; and for bedrooms, the Yorkshire materials known as taffeta or glace.

Curtains.—It has somehow come to be an article of faith with the ordinary upholsterer that curtains, under whatever circumstances, should be made of figured materials. There are many reasons, however, in favour of plain materials. There are good reasons for decorating the ceiling and the frieze with designs, and beyond doubt a pattern on a wall is constantly advantageous, and helps, for example, to furnish the room of the young couple who start in life without pictures. To have a plain carpet, the housewife says, is most trying: every footfall shows. We are, therefore, fast arriving at a fashion of "patterning" everything—a most undesirable condition of things. Now, a plain curtain, falling into good folds, offers itself as an agreeable rest to the eye. Moreover, the best materials, and those which fall into the best folds, are the plain ones. Their severity may be mitigated by borders, and by varied trimming, and pleasant gradation of colouring can be so introduced much more easily when you are not hampered by a figured material. Cloth is, perhaps, the best material possible, but there are many which afford abundant variety.

Wall Ornaments.—I have lately endeavoured, on the wall of the Walker Art Gallery (in Liverpool), to show how many things may be used decoratively upon a wall besides pictures. I trust it may not be too severe to say that the bulk of householders know little about good art, and could not pay for it if they did; and we are purposely talking about the average Briton. It would, therefore, be greatly to his advantage if he could be induced not to buy second-rate pictures, but to wait until his purse and knowledge justify his buying good ones, and meanwhile to ornament his walls with such things as small Chippendale mirrors, hammered brass sconces, plaster casts after the antique and Donatello, blue china on shelves or brackets, little eighteenth-century engravings by Bartolozzi, feather fans, little objects of natural history, such as a fine Peruvian butterfly, &c. &c., all of which add interest and gaiety to a room in a greater degree than any pictures, and are a thousand times better than second-rate or bad ones. Nothing can compensate for having indifferent art presented to us day by day, and it is certain that the very feeble admiration generally exhibited for engravings after Gainsborough, Reynolds, and Turner, &c., is largely due to the demoralising influence of the prosaic, humdrum landscapes from Academies and Water-Colour Societies—Royal and otherwise—and the excessive prominence given in our sitting-rooms to photographs of modern life and photographic portraits of our friends. Compared with such pictures, the lid of an old brass warming-pan is a fine ornament, and a "long-lady" blue jar becomes absolutely classic.

Furniture.—It is pleasing to turn to the illustrated books of furniture of the last century, commencing with Copeland in 1746; Chippendale, 1754; Ince and Mayhew, about 1760; Matthias Darley, 1763; Heppelwhite, 1789; Sheraton, 1791, and see how excellent a school they initiated. Up to that time, furniture was architectonic and clumsy, the chair, table, and bureau of the Stuart period being as ponderous, immovable, and unhandy as it is possible to imagine; picturesque, occasionally, as a "property" for an artist, but as furniture to live amongst and to use, quite outrageous. No doubt the men I have mentioned did indeed copy their designs from the French, for Chippendale has been tracked, and we know the source of almost all his designs; but in practice, however absurd some of their illustrations, a characteristic English sobriety comes in and modifies the excess of the volatile Frenchman with admirable results. How far we might have developed, no one can say; but towards the end of the century the French Revolution stopped the supply of illustrated books from France, and after that—the deluge.

We feel the weakness of these cabinetmakers and carvers, as we read the prefaces of their books, and the titles of some of their plates. For vulgar and pretentious bombast, it is difficult to find their parallel; and much as we extol and copy Chippendale, there can be little or no doubt that he was as ignorant and pretentious a fellow as ever hawked his wares, and Sheraton was very nearly as bad. They could get along while they had good copies; but, like all mere copyists, when left to themselves, they were impotent, and produced the character-less rubbish of our grandfathers' time, from which we have only lately escaped; indeed, we are not fully free of it yet. Their furniture, how-ever, under French influence, has come to be highly valued, and is being largely restored and copied, greatly to the general advantage; for the best of the work of that period—say in France, 1650 to the Revolution, and in England, 1730 to the Revolution—is beyond dis-pute the finest furniture the world has ever produced.

Chapter 6
Fabrics

Some years ago, I read a paper to the Architectural Institute upon "Hangings," which contained a most elementary description of a variety of useful fabrics, and the yarns from which they were made; and it was amusing to read in one of the daily papers that "it would be well if Peter Robinson's young men could read Mr. Heaton's address." No doubt the remark was intended to be complimentary to me, but it mainly showed that others had noticed what I had long been aware of: that the shopkeeper's assistant is profoundly ignorant of the nature and constituents of ordinary fabrics.

If you go into a Yorkshire mill, and produce specimens of fabrics which are interesting or uncommon, there are two or three simple tests at once resorted to, in order to explain their nature. The first is commonly the tongue: wool and cotton reveal their nature much more plainly when wet than when dry. The next is fire: upon application of a lighted match you at once distinguish between animal substances and vegetable; the former burn to a cinder, the latter to an ash, like paper. The fingers, also, reveal much when a person is experienced in fabrics. The nose tells a little more: linen, for instance, rarely loses its distinctive smell, even after many years. In a London shop, none of these tests are resorted to; and your ordinary shopkeeper's assistant is generally entirely in the dark as to the nature of the fabrics he is selling.

And, as it is the study of a great many manufacturers to hide the cheap materials of a fabric behind the costlier ones, to pretend, in fact, that the cheap materials do not exist, it is little wonder that the amateur is completely deceived.

It will therefore be well to ascertain carefully the nature of the most useful fibres, and by that means to arrive at the characteristics of the fabrics produced from them.

There is no use talking of "good fabrics" and "bad fabrics"; the only profitable question is their suitability to the uses we make of them. Perhaps there is no more rubbishy-looking fabric produced than what is called "scrim"; but the man who has to line a rough wall, knows perfectly well that scrim is a really good article when so used. In the same way, the poor miserable fabric called "butter-cloth" is well suited for the wrapping up of butter, and is as good for the purpose as paper is bad. The mischief steps in when people attempt to make curtains of scrim, or dresses of butter-cloth. A few years ago, some of the ladies who commenced the School of Needlework in Kensington, set the fashion of using Bolton sheeting for dresses—and even for embroidered dresses. No doubt there is a proper use for Bolton sheeting, though it may not yet have been found out—unless it be to make sheets for paupers; but a viler misuse of a fabric than to make it carry embroidery for dresses was surely never conceived.

As it is impossible to go through all known fabrics, and to inquire into all their uses, we can only attempt to examine the more common and the more useful, especially in regard to the substance from which they are made.

The exasperating fashion which has set in of late years, to have everything at an almost impossible price, has further muddled us in a question of which most of us were sufficiently ignorant; for now it has become necessary for the manufacturer who has looms to keep going, to make linen appear like silk, cotton like wool, jute like linen; to hide threads which form the substance of the fabric, behind others and costlier ones which form its surface—and so, if possible, to deceive even the very elect.

Cotton.—Cotton is no doubt the fibre which mankind first made use of for woven fabrics. The history of the early stages is buried in obscurity, and certainly it is quite antecedent to any known literature. Specimens are to be seen of cotton fabric produced at least four thousand years before the Christian era—such as pieces of mummy cloth. Indeed, though a great many ancient manufactures are made of linen, considering that parts of India and Egypt were settled, and, so to speak, civilised countries long before these Western lands, there can be little doubt that cotton fabrics are the earliest productions. But whichever it be, cotton or linen, is little to our present purpose. Both of them are very long in the fibre compared with wool, and entirely without spring and elasticity. Crush or pinch either of them, and it assumes and retains the bent and crushed form so obtained, in contrast to the behaviour of an animal fibre, which springs back into its original form. Now this is an exceedingly important element in these vegetable fibres. If the use to which you apply them demands that they should hang in good folds, and have natural spring in them to retain these folds when crushed or crumpled, clearly they are inadequate. They are, for the most part, cheap fibres, and their length of "staple" (as it is termed, alluding to the natural length of the growth) adds greatly to the strength of the yarn produced from them; and in this respect they have always an advantage over short-staple fibres.

The fibre of cotton, in its manner of growth, is quite straight, has none of the wriggle or wave of wool, and is kept straight in spinning. Its chief utility for better and more valuable fabrics is that of forming a cheap and useful warp (the lengthway threads of a fabric); and as it makes an exceedingly strong thread, owing to its evenness and length of staple, it must always form a most useful and desirable fibre for that purpose. Unfortunately, its cheapness tempts the competing manufacturer to use it for weft also (the cross-way threads), and so used, its inferiority to animal fibres becomes apparent, for it is entirely free from lustre, and absolutely flaccid and without spring.

Consequently, however useful it may be in its place, it is certain to depreciate those fabrics where lustre and spring are essential.

You will see from these remarks that cotton, apart from the question of warmth, must always be amongst the inferior and less valuable of fibres; and when one considers how largely the question of warmth for dress and hangings, in the northern countries, affects our view of the value of a woven fabric, its undesirability compared with the majority of our better materials will be seen at once; and when competition assists in making it used when it ought not to be used, its cheapness is a snare of the greatest magnitude.

The question of utility must not be forgotten. Short-sighted people will go about saying (when warned that a fabric will not wear), "Oh, it will last long enough for me." But there inevitably comes a day of retribution; and it is not to the credit of any of us, still less to the credit of decent housewifery, that we should encourage the use of a fabric which will not wear a reasonable time. There is sure to be a day of recrimination and repentance, when one has allowed a bad article to be used. People are well aware of this when they come to the constructional questions of a building. Architects do not build with a brick or a slate which is only to last two or three years—or even with a plaster which will crumble within the same time: the weakness is too evident, and the consequent regret and ill-repute too immediate. But people will constantly use woven fabrics which their own sense tells them, let alone the warning of a conscientious salesman, will be shabby in a twelvemonth.

And any dyer, and any shopkeeper even, knows quite well that a fibre of cotton will not take dye at all well. There are one or two exceptions to this rule, as in the case of Turkey red and indigo—and possibly the dyes obtainable from "cachou." But for all that, the rule holds good that cotton receives dye badly; therefore salesmen should advise people that a fabric which has its main surface of cotton should be used only sparingly when dyed. In printed work this remark does not apply equally, because the mordants used in printing are so much more reliable and serviceable than any dyeing. Its true service-ableness is in its natural white, or creamy white state.

Even two or three years ago, French commercial travellers, who came over selling fabrics in this country, used to say as a recommen-dation "It is all wool," or, "All wool and silk." Lately this remark has been entirely dropped, because the fabrics they now bring are half, or nine-tenths, or entirely, cotton. Ask them about the permanence of these, and they have not a word to say. They shrug their shoulders and say, "Monsieur, it is what is wanted." And these remarks apply to all the vegetable fibres.

Linen.—Linen is a fibre of a still longer staple than cotton; but it is relatively clumsy, and never loses, however much it is handled, a certain stiffness. Now, this quality makes it valuable for sheets and towels, and the napery of the table; but in price it cannot compete with cotton, and its uses are much more limited. It is exceedingly strong and enduring, and it is only when manufacturers use it to supersede wool, wishing the unwary to mistake its stiffness for the spring and firmness of wool, that its undesirability is discovered. If people, in buying fabrics in shops, would take the simple precaution to light a lucifer-match and test the nature of the fibre (animal or vegetable) where there is any doubt, they would hold manufacturers in check about this false use of linen.

Perhaps, in linen, the undesirability of using things out of their proper sphere is most apparent. For warm or temperate climates its smooth and almost lustre-like surface, forming the very best of con-ductors, makes it feel, as we see in sheets and table-linen, agreeably cool to the touch. And here is its greatest value; but its stiffness and comparative coarseness will always render it one of the least used of our fibres.

Silk.—Silk must have been used in very early times; and, being an article of Oriental production, it may have been used as early as cotton. As an animal production, it at once attains a value, which is increased by a lustre such as never belongs to vegetable fibres. But its principal characteristic is the smallness of the fibre, which can be best understood by stating that about seventy-five miles of it only weighs one ounce.

"Net" Silk.—As a first process in the manipulation, the cocoon is thrown into hot water, and is then fingered and rolled round, and otherwise slightly rubbed, until the outside end frees itself from the rest; and the manipulators then pass it over a wheel or spindle, and in this way the original filament of the silkworm is obtained free. But, owing to its exceeding smallness, four of these threads are usually wound together; and the thread generally used by the embroiderer is formed of at least twenty of the silk-worm's threads. This gives some idea of its exceeding smallness. It is flaccid, and, for the most part, springless, except when used in considerable bulk; but, as we all know, it has a beautiful lustre, and may be called the prince of fibres, from an ornamental point of view.

"Spun" Silk.—A broad distinction must be drawn between silk, called in trade "net" silk (the thread of the silk-worm), and "spun" silk, which is composed of the spoilt cocoons, either where the worm has died inside, or has eaten its way out, in which cases the cocoon could not be wound off. It is entirely a modern idea to utilise these dead or spoilt cocoons; and the result must never be confounded with the silk-worm's filament. The manufacturing process is as follows: The whole of these inferior or spoilt cocoons are softened by boiling, and then pulled out anyhow into a factitious thread, including even the very body of the worm itself; so that if you come across a silk fabric which seems unusually heavy at a moderate price, you may know at once that it is this inferior silk. Naturally, it is always irregular and full of lumps and rubbish, the silk fibres not lying all one way, as they ought to do, but in a tangle and mess. Its price may be considered, for our present purpose, as not more than one-fourth of "net" silk. No

doubt it has its uses, but they are comparatively few compared with those of the real article; and it should always be borne in mind that from the nature of the yarns so made, dirt is rapidly accumulated. Witness the modern questionable use of it in the form of plush to illustrate this. It is always a source of regret to find how far embroiderers consent to use it, in the form of filoselle. Hence comes a great deal of the thoroughly inferior embroidery of the present day, subordinate as compared with old Italian or Spanish work, which was always made from the silk-worm's filament.

The manufacture of this filament is expressed in the trade by the word "throwing"; the factitious thread that I have been discussing is known as "spun"; and the throwster and spinner are, in manufacturing districts, engaged in entirely different trades.

"Thrown" silk is occasionally required as fine as four of the silkworm's filaments. "Spun" silk is more the thickness of eighty to a hundred. Think of the superiority of an old Lyons velvet to modern plush, and you have the difference between the two well accentuated.

Wool.—It is difficult for the inhabitants of a cold or temperate climate to assume on these questions the feelings of an Oriental, but as Europeans, we think naturally of wool as of far the most valuable fibre we have. It came into use later than cotton, but there is no profit in endeavouring to ascertain how much later.

There is a broad distinction to be made between wools, or, to use the trade phrase, between "worsted" and woollen." It is a distinction that has arisen from our manner of manipulating it, and from the length of the growth, but it is still a very broad, useful distinction; and it is necessary to understand it, because there is the utmost confusion here in the south of England with regard to it. In the manufacturing parts of Yorkshire, the seat of the trade in both, every apprentice boy knows the meaning of that distinction.

Fine wool, grown in the hotter climates of the world, has a natural wriggle or wave in it; while *hair*, like our own, is, for the most part, straight, so that the black song which speaks of "the wool on the top of his head" has more truth than might appear at first.

All the wools of the colder climates are straight, and of the nature of our own hair. Goat's hair, the wools of Iceland and Russian sheep, the north of England wool, and many other sorts, are all straight, or if they have a wave, have very little—certainly nothing which can be called a wriggle. Many of these fibres are at least six inches in length, some longer; while the wool of the more southern countries, South-downs of England, Saxony, and especially Australia, are full of wriggle, and they are seldom more than one-third of the length of the hairy wools which we have been speaking of, and are often only one inch in length.

Now, when these northern wools come to be manipulated, they are kept straight during all the processes of spinning, and, somehow or other, have come to be called "worsted." It is said that this word is derived from the name of a little town in Norfolk, to which Flemish spinners and weavers emigrated, and used these very wools; but the accuracy of this explanation may be doubted.

The short and fine wools have too much wriggle in them, and are too short in staple to be so treated, and they are spun without any at-tention to the position of the fibres, which curl round each other, and "felt" together in the manipulation, and are popularly called "wool-len." The difference between these two processes will be found, on consideration, to be immense. The "woollen" is used for most of our clothing, and blankets, and the things that we require for warmth. The "worsted" is a much better conductor, and so is not suitable for this purpose.

As regards value, however, the worsted is considerably in advance of the other. Goat's hair fetches ordinarily two shillings per pound—partly, no doubt, from its beautiful gloss and spring—while wool has been sent into Liverpool for sale, of which the staple was so exceed-ingly short, although beautifully fine, that having been knocked down at auction at two-pence per pound, the buyer found it would not pay to expend the railway fare for removing it, and it was left in the docks for years. That, no doubt, is an extreme case; but it will serve to show how these fibres sell according to the length of staple. Not that we wish to depreciate the value of woollen yarns for a moment; all men's clothing, and cloth generally, and flannel, and blankets, and things necessary to our comfort, are woollen.

Alpaca.—On the other hand, the fibre called Alpaca or Llama forms a fabric which is generally pronounced the *most* beautiful. The alpaca is the South American form of the camel,—which shows how animals, separated by one of our primeval changes of the earth, may develop in two different directions, the hair of the Oriental camel being vastly inferior.

Mohair.—Next to this in beauty and utility comes the hair of the Syrian goat, which Mr. Holman Hunt has delineated in "The Scape-goat." We usually speak of it under the name of "mohair"; but it is quite distinct from alpaca, though often confused by name in the shops. These hairs (they are called "hair" in the market) and the long wool of the north of England, Scotland, and to some extent Iceland and Russia, possess the valuable quality called "lustre" or gloss, a character much valued; but which, of course, is absent in the short wools of which clothing is made.

Adulteration.—Now it will be evident here that these fibres which, on the average, may be priced, when worked up into yarn, at least two shillings per pound, are readily adulterated with cotton, which is about sixpence per pound, to the great deterioration of a large number of fabrics, and to the deception of the public generally. For wool contains springiness, and gloss, and warmth-bearing qualities, while cotton is entirely without these; and we ought to learn to detect the presence of cotton in these fabrics, since the temptation to use it as an adulteration is evident. To such an extent is this done, even with silk, that cotton is used, mingled with silk, in order to lower the price;

and many a lady who thinks she buys a silk dress, gets one that is one-third cotton. The burning test at once reveals this. In buying a silk dress, light a Lucifer match and see how it burns— whether like paper or like wool.

It is worthy of observation here, that silk, owing to its great value, has been adulterated in another way, namely, by the addition of sugar of lead, in the trade called "weighted"; but, fortunately for the general public, the sugar of lead burns like paper; and where a great deal of it has been introduced, the whole fabric burns like paper, giving one the impression that there is no silk in it whatever; and even now preparations are being made to manufacture a so-called silk yarn out of wood fibre. Verily "all men are liars."

Jute is a fibre derived from a plant analogous to linen. It is perhaps best described as a very coarse, strong linen, with all the strength, and even more length of staple than linen. It is only worthy of mention because of the tendency to cheapen material, which has made it a sort of coarse substitute for the other vegetable fibres. It seems to have no beauty whatever; but may be useful enough in the form of packing canvas, and, at any rate, it employs a considerable number of Dundee spinners and weavers.

WOVEN FABRICS

Tapestry.—To turn to the woven material. We should never lose sight of the splendid fabric of tapestry, at all events in these countries, Belgium, England, Spain, France, where we have learnt to know the beauty of it. It is, beyond all others, a fabric which Mr. Ruskin would call "noble"; but it is unnecessary to cover it here, because of its costliness. It is scarcely a "practical question of the hour." More essential are the fabrics made in looms, which we all buy, and which are in daily use. Old tapestries had generally a warp of cotton or linen, well embedded in cross threads, which were invariably worsted.

Velvets.—Next after tapestry we must place velvet, not for its general utility, but for the beauty of the production. When one reflects on the velvets of Genoa and Venice, often figured, and containing threads of gold and silver, it is impossible not to be conscious of the beauty of the manufacture, although here again the warp was usually cotton. Today, nobody seems willing to buy anything but cheap imitations of them.

The velvet woven from mohair, or mohair and wool (on a cotton warp again), and generally known as Utrecht velvet, produced both in Germany and in the north of France, and now by Lister of Bradford, must not be forgotten; and though it can scarcely be called beautiful, it is undoubtedly a most useful and excellent fabric. So much is this article in request, that the utmost ingenuity has been brought to bear upon the production of it; and some clever fellow has found that the right way is to weave two pieces together, face to face, where the threads forming the pile are automatically cut, and the one piece in the loom comes out as two pieces in the hand. There is a shockingly bad edition of this article, which bears the suspicious name of "plushette," and may be best described as an admirably designed dust-trap; and by way of keeping up the modern fashion for adulteration, velvet has also been made from jute, of which the best that can be said is that it is not so nasty as one might expect. And for those who like cheap and showy rubbish, there is velveteen, used as a groundwork for printed curtains. Though showy and fine in texture, it seems to have resulted in a fabric which is at once entirely flaccid, a quick fader, and an effectual catcher of dirt. It is a prominent instance of unconscientiousness in modern trade. Plain velveteen for dresses, which are probably only wanted for ephemeral use, is admissible, and probably a useful article.

After these come damasks; and (velvet alone possibly an exception) silk damask is the most beautiful fabric made, especially when the warp and weft are both alike of "net" silk. The resource shown in the patterning of this fabric is beyond all praise for artistic ability. Probably the most beautiful fabrics in the world come under this head; but the cost will always keep the production of them comparatively small.

Satin Laine et Soie.—Now, if the surface be kept entirely silk, there is no objection to a backing of worsted; and in the north of France large quantities are made of a fabric entirely silk on the face, and entirely worsted behind. The silk in this article is only spun silk, but there must be cheap fabrics produced for shallow purses; and this article was undeniably good until some one, in an excessive zeal for low prices, did his best to spoil it by changing the worsted at the back to cotton (without saving a sixth of the whole price), and thereby producing an article which could only be called rubbish. Fortunately, the public may be warned by the almost satirical name given to it— "silk sheeting."

Modern competition here again continues to spoil a good article. The silk damask which covered the walls of an Italian palace was entirely "net" or "thrown" silk. The silk damask made for today's trade is nearly all cotton—cotton in the warp, and partly cotton in the weft. The lucifer match (and which of us does not carry lucifer matches nowadays?) will detect the cotton at once.

Lustrous Yorkshire Goods.—Next in value to these come a number of Yorkshire fabrics (which are woven from long-haired, springy worsted), whether for beauty or utility—utility both for dress, for curtains, for wall coverings, for summer clothing, and numberless other necessities of life. We speak of them as worsted satins, camlets, moreens, diagonals, &c., all made from long wool, and occasionally goat's hair. If to hang in fine folds is a merit in such articles (and who can doubt it?), these fabrics unquestionably carry the day over everything else. No fabric made of yarn with the flaccidity of cotton or linen can be compared with them. The only thing remotely equal to them in this respect is woollen cloth, and there you at once start without the lustre.

Utility.—We cannot here include questions of the loom, but mention must be made of another result of competition—the destruction of the *usefulness* of fabrics. Ordinary weaving is, of course, over one, under one; and all pattern weaving is a series of varieties from this, whether it be a simple twill, which is over two, under one, of the weft, or other small variations which are quite consistent with the production of a good fabric. When, however, we come to the use of the Jacquard machine, the temptation is to take great liberties with this arrangement, and, roughly speaking, to go under one, over ten, and the result is a poor fabric. This should never be forgotten, because, once let a fabric become loose in the construction, and its life, in reasonable condition, becomes exceedingly short. This applies particularly to figured fabrics with a good deal of cotton in them and very little silk. They may be filled with gum or size to make them passably saleable, while fresh from the loom; but hang such a material up as curtains, or make it into ladies' dresses, or hang it as wall drapery, and you have a fabric which soon begins to lose its integrity, and becomes shabby and worthless in an incredibly short time.

Carpets.—It is undoubtedly difficult to discuss carpets in the limited space of an essay. Every one knows the beauty of an Oriental carpet, not alone the costly carpets made, probably, at the order of a potentate whose palace was gilded, or the exquisite work done, five centuries ago, with silk pile (the best of which were made by refugees in Poland), but the ordinary carpet, common throughout Asia, and down to the shores of the Bosphorus, distinguished, not alone for beauty of design, but almost equally for beauty of colour, and for technical skill in the manufacture. The clever and skilful way in which these carpets have their pile arranged slightly on the slant (which is preserved continuously throughout the life of the carpet), places them at once, irrespective of their beautiful colouring and design, ahead of our modern productions; for the modern pile carpet has the exceedingly bad fault of its pile becoming crushed in this direction or the other, and so producing ugly places, which look as if they had been damaged. The Oriental pile, on the other hand, always slopes —however much worn it may become—in the way in which the weaver gave it its original cast. Perhaps, we shall have to content ourselves with picking the old ones up now and again for the well-to-do, a restoration of this work being impracticable. But the drop is terrible when one comes to consider the modern carpet—for instance, that of Kidderminster—which, indeed, does not merit any consideration at all. The Brussels carpet may have been a good fabric twenty years ago, when its thick threads were made of good, long-haired Yorkshire wool, but modern competition has reduced the thickness of the thread and the staple of wool to such an extent that a Brussels carpet will not last *one season* in a London club. And the article is so well known, and buyers are so accustomed to it at a low price, that it is useless to endeavour to return to the old quality.

Patent Axminster.—It seems that the imitation Axminster carpet of Templeton and other makers is by far the best fabric in the market. It is made of worsted chenille, the chenille being prepared beforehand, and all the colours being woven in their proper places by the Jacquard, or an equivalent machine. The chenille is woven on a cotton warp, and the backing-threads, which form the body of the carpet, are either jute or coarse worsted. Now, the chenille makes a complete surface, and unless some fool gets at the backing-threads with a penknife, the foot never touches anything but the pile, and nothing else is exposed to wear. So long as this condition of things holds, it is difficult to see what is to wear them out. They may get dirty, of course; but destruction, in the ordinary sense of the phrase,—"wear and tear," is impossible. It has the very serious defect just now mentioned: that of the pile lying in varying directions instead of all one way; but no doubt some clever head will some day remedy this defect.

The carpet known as Wilton has, in a measure, the same qualities, though not woven of chenille, the top of the pile alone being exposed to wear. But it shows every seam plainly, and is entirely lacking in that sense of breadth and compactness of surface which we expect in a carpet.

Cloth.—There remain last, but not least, the multitude of very useful fabrics made of woollen weft, as distinguished from worsted, and more or less associated under the name of "cloth." Some of them, under the head of serge, are thoroughly good, hanging in good folds, and wearing for years. The pity of it is that they have been cheapened by the introduction of a cotton warp; and little by little the deterioration of this fabric has gone on, until the lower qualities are valueless; but on worsted warps they are thoroughly good.

Of cloth proper there is an enormous variety. The article (in the processes to which it is subjected) becomes very much felted, and is then an impervious fabric. The felting may be done to a great extent, or a smaller one, as desired. For certain purposes, as, for instance, the overcoat of a driver who wants it to turn rain, it can scarcely be over-done. For draperies, curtains, grounds for embroidery, &c., it should be done comparatively slightly, so as still to exhibit its construction quite plainly. It gains, however, sufficient firmness by a very moderate amount of felting to fall into most excellent folds.

Character.—And this brings us to the question of what may be called "character" in woven fibres. A proportion of people, among whom architects are prominent, like to see the threads of a fabric. They feel, which is no doubt true, that there is an element of deception and pretense about a fabric whose threads are invisible, where the whole construction is hidden beneath an artificially raised nap (as in the cloth which men wear in the evening), or in a mere fuzzle like a felt; and they would like to see the construction of the thing. But the difficulty is that a still larger number of people (among whom the fair sex is prominent) like to see everything as fine as possible; and this also suits the book of the shopkeeper, for a fine-looking article at the money is like good wine, it "needs no bush." But these two demands are inconsistent with each other. If the demand for a visible construction only went the length of excluding felts and fine satins of cotton or worsted, there would be no harm done; but we have always to bear in mind that cloth, which is an excellent article, has been for centuries made with a raised or dressed surface, hiding the construction, and still, in spite of it, remains a most excellent fabric. The Orientals have been most successful in the production of fabrics which, while showing the construction plainly enough, still look good and handsome. And no doubt, if we all set the example of demanding such fabrics, Leeds would soon provide home-made things with that character—a cloth which they say in the market "shows its bones." In Italy, the usual covering of a horse which brings a light cart to market is a cloth that is almost entirely without nap, generally of a pale scarlet; and as facilities for intercommunication improve, no doubt the Italians will bring this material to our market. The French red army-cloth seems a happy medium; the raising, if there be any, being exceedingly moderate.

Muslin.—It is difficult to speak of the question of muslins, their uses are so various and their prices so moderate; but they have furnished us of late years with the Swiss Leno curtain, which seems to me entirely abominable, and the figured muslin called "Madras," of which the principal characteristic is that it gathers dirt at an unprecedented pace. If people want summer curtains of a thin material, they should be content with the muslin plain.

Chintz.—We now come to an important article of modern industry —Chintz. The Indian prints of a century ago, going more or less under the name of "Palampore," though on thin white cotton ground (entirely cotton), are so exceedingly beautiful (or were) that they must not be forgotten. The trade still continues at Cawnpore and elsewhere up to the present day, in a cheap and less desirable form, but still with much merit. They are now printed, at a low price, on rough native cotton, and gain by the use of that ground, the whites being more ivory-like, something between the shade of dark ivory and salmon. We have no English or French production to compare with them, and if the designs were better adapted to our modern wants, we should see this article in great demand. But the patterns are immensely large, and, as a matter of workmanship, very badly printed. The old goods of this character, produced a hundred years ago, were far better in workmanship, and on an absolutely white ground, which, with its accompaniment of fineness and mechanical regularity, makes us suspect that the cloth was sent out in the days of John Company to be printed in India. A specimen was sent some years ago to be examined at the school of design at Lahore, and it came back ticketed with the remark, "Lahore work; one hundred or one hundred and twenty years old; partly hand-painted." In the centre, at the lower part of this curtain, was a sort of ornamental hill, which was filled with birds and lions and various other creatures; and from this there grew a tree with fine foliage, which filled up the rest of the curtain as far as the borders —a most beautiful production, at once bright in colour and not in the least gaudy. Needless to say, they must have had a costly and complete set of blocks (probably one hundred and fifty) to produce a single curtain.

After seeing such a fabric, one looks with contempt and pity upon our modern chintzes. Notwithstanding these beautiful productions spoken of, there is no doubt that chintz printing suffers greatly from being relegated to a cheap cotton ground. Of course, there are uses for a chintz on a cheap cotton ground; but it is to be hoped that there will arise a demand for chintz (especially for use in large towns) on a worsted ground. The writer has seen chintz taken off the foot of an old wooden bed, which had been there ninety years, a Yorkshire worsted fabric (moreen), and printed at Swaislands in Kent, at the end of the last century, and still in good condition. We only want some spirited person to put fine designs into chintz-printing, and print them on a worsted ground—some William Morris of his day— to find out how much we lose by relegating chintz to a shilling a yard for bedrooms.

We have very much to learn in fabrics from the Oriental nations. Apart from the question of fineness (which they can manage when they wish), they have several fabrics more or less known under the name of "Kelim," which have a distinctly handsome coarseness, and which, even in the eyes of the European, are not looked down upon as being necessarily of low value. Our modern European manufactures are certainly entirely deficient in this class of fabric.

It is to be hoped that the modern demand for adulterated fabrics may wear itself out; (for dress fabrics it does not matter so much, because their use is ephemeral; and ladies may always be trusted, I think, not to buy a thoroughly bad fabric—twice), and that before long the fashion may change in favour of more genuine materials, and especially in favour of printing beautiful designs on worsted grounds, —a method calculated to produce, at a most moderate price, an article of great beauty and great durability. And there is no difficulty in colouring such a ground by the aid of a stencil plate, adding varied and beautiful colour to a fine design.

Use.—As to the fitting use of these fabrics, there is no need to recommend people to buy curtains—that is a foregone conclusion; but a word may be said respecting what is termed a "valance," which, in the hands of most people, is simply a snare. No doubt two curtains to a window, when drawn back during the day, without any connecting feature, do often look excessively severe and bare; but good taste will always come to the rescue in making this otherwise useless and solely aesthetic feature, a valance, moderate, both in style and dimensions. But curtains, however ornamental in adding to the pleasing form and colour of a room, too often all come at one end or one side; and if they are in contrast of colour to the wall, care should be taken to carry their form and colour to the other sides if possible. And here the portiere, which has also the advantage of appearing to be a shield from draughts, comes in most usefully. A drapery to an overmantel might be equally comely and advantageous. But the housewife's horror of dust seems generally a complete bar to the use of wall draperies hanging in folds. When so used they are always picturesque and comfortable-looking; and such draperies do not gather dust in anything approaching the degree in which window-curtains do. Draughts come through window-sashes, bringing dust with them, but no draught comes through a wall. In rooms where bareness and a mechanical hardness have been a prominent feature, a dado of mohair velvet, about three feet high, has been used with the most excellent result. This hung loose in folds, by rings and studs, from a moulded dado rail, and divided up into shortish lengths, answering to the breaks in the wall, is easy to remove and shake; and the housewife's care for dust has been cajoled for the moment.

But it is for the sanctuaries of churches that more hangings are principally wanted. The objection generally taken is that such work is not permanent, would be a care, would require replacement, &c., all of which, it may be remarked, applies in even a still greater degree to altar-cloths and vestments, which are not thereby prohibited. The cloth sanctuary-hangings of St. Alban's Church, Holborn, after twenty-five years of use, were still in good condition; and if architects would specify such hangings with as much care for the quality and material to be employed, as they expend upon the brick, stone, or slate of the fabric, there is no reason why they should not last fifty years, by which time even wooden benches, hot-water pipes, and lead lattices usually want a good overhauling.

A large proportion of the lower part of a sanctuary is nearly always hard, bare, and featureless; and not only will hangings introduce colour and softness and variety of form, which are, beyond all things, desirable, but they will also add a sense that the Presence Chamber is furnished and cared for, a sense which no carving and painting at ten times the cost can half so well achieve.

Chapter 7
Furniture and Decoration
of the 18th Century

Carlyle has said that the eighteenth century produced nothing of value but the French Revolution; he might, also, have excepted English furniture.

It appears to require about a century for the great wheel of fashion to make one complete revolution. We can see that what our great-grandfathers bought and valued (1750 to 1790); what our grandfathers despised and neglected (1790 to 1820); what our fathers utterly forgot (1820 to 1850), we value, restore, and copy!

The furniture of the latter half of the last century—at any rate, the best specimens of it—has, of late, so commonly come to be regarded as the best the world has yet produced, that no apology seems needed for an inquiry into the circumstances of its origin and development.

We are not here concerned with remarkable, historical, and priceless pieces of furniture made for princes and millionaires. These have been well illustrated by the works of Jacquemart, Viollet-le-Duc, Havard, and others; and museums not only abound in such specimens, but seem for the most part to exhibit no others—reminding one strongly of the ordinary history of the past, which begins and ends with accounts of kings, councillors, and generals; while in these democratic days we rather prefer to hear about the people and their doings. So here I propose to discuss and illustrate the ordinary chair, table, and cabinet, designed for, and especially adapted to, the daily use of the average Anglo-Saxon; and, so considered, there is nothing to compete with the best of what we call "Chippendale" furniture. And we may see reasons for it not far to seek. Men of genius and education in art did not consider it beneath them to design and ornament furniture for the average citizen—witness such names as Vanbrugh, Chambers, Adam, Cipriani, Pergolesi, Angelica Kauffman; and even Sheraton, with all his vulgar pomposity, was a far superior man to our modern furniture designers. In France, Louis XIV and his minister Colbert had established (1664) a Royal Academy of Painting, Architecture, and Sculpture; and Lebrun the painter was attached to it, to provide fine designs for furniture; whilst in England (following France, as usual, a century later) the rapid spread of comparative wealth to a greatly enlarged class of the community had opened the door at once to good design and good workmanship for common articles of daily use.

The desire to possess fine chairs, sideboards, and cabinets, of the style we know as "Chippendale," "Adams,"[3] or "Sheraton," has spread to such a large proportion of educated and well-to-do people, that it may safely be said that the best of those productions are sold daily at quite three times their original cost; and though this, and far more than this, may be said of many things which come to the hammer at "Christie's," yet, in the case of this eighteenth century furniture, it is not merely rare and historical pieces that fetch good prices, but the rank and file of all the best work of the two Chippendales, Sheraton, Heppelwhite, or Shearer, or even articles supposed to have been designed by the brothers Adam, Richardson, and the small army of their imitators. And this is not on special occasions and at favourite auction rooms alone, but everywhere, all over the land—wherever good things are appreciated.

We feel the bulk of this furniture to be at once good to look at, useful for daily life, constructively excellent, and within the reach of the average purse; and we have come to understand, very certainly, the clumsiness and impracticability of the Stuart furniture of the seventeenth century, the grossly false taste and ugliness of the productions of the last two reigns, and the weakness and want of character of a so-called "Early English" fad of our own times; and, by contrast, good "Chippendale" furniture, even when badly notched and somewhat worm-eaten, appears most excellent and desirable. Beyond doubt, a considerable number of London cabinetmakers have been employed, for some years past, in restoring and reproducing it.

It is pleasant to think of it as a distinctly English style, for it became so as its development proceeded; but its origin is beyond doubt *French*—French of the period of Louis Quatorze, and not in any sense a development from the English furniture of Queen Elizabeth and the Stuarts. We borrowed it from France during that most remarkable period when France, under Louis XIV, was engaged in inaugurating a new era in the development of art—a movement which placed her in the van of civilised nations, in all matters relating to the housing of the wealthy—in advance of Italy, the source of all these arts; and in a position which she has maintained, at least up to the Revolution, if not indeed to the present time.

But, having borrowed it, the natural sobriety of the English turn of mind toned down its eccentricities, stiffened its curves, and added an air of severity; while the French went on developing it in the other direction, until the French parentage of the English branch has become all but invisible, and we regard it as a style of our own.

Anyone, however, who will take the trouble to study the historical development of furniture at a good museum, may soon see the marked contrast between the forms of English furniture of the seventeenth century, nearly always architectural—pilaster, shaft, arcade —and the graceful and flowing lines of the work produced in 1730 and onwards. Wherever the architectural forms were deserted, sweeps and curves were introduced, the originals of which may invariably be found in work of a century or more earlier from Italy, Germany, Flanders, and France, but mostly from France.

Chippendale was, in the first place, and principally, a carver—a maker of extravagant and flamboyant frames to mirrors and girandoles; and so eagerly did he copy the original, that he actually seems to have outdone the French upon their own ground.

But when one looks at the all-but-unbridged gulf which seemed, thirty years ago, to separate us from the daily life, from the furniture designers and cabinetmakers of Germany, Italy, and France, it seems at first sight puzzling that W. Jones in 1739, Copeland in 1746, Thomas Chippendale in 1754, and Ince and Mayhew probably[4] only a year or two later, should suddenly have appeared with large folio and quarto books of costly copper and steel engravings, with all the signs of a full-blown "style" about them, and that in contrast, rather than otherwise, to the existing style of this country.

Later on, we had good designers, men of superior cultivation and opportunities, who spoke French, travelled to Rome and Greece, and published books of design, two or three of them in French as well as English—Sir William Chambers (by no means always good), 1760; the brothers Adam[5], 1773, et seq.; George Richardson, 1781; Pergolesi, 1777, et seq.; Cipriani, 1786. But previous to 1739, judging by such books as exist, no English designer seems to have published anything worthy of notice.

How, then, did Chippendale, and his fellow cabinetmakers, or perhaps, to speak more correctly, their predecessors, arrive at their Louis Quatorze style?

In these days of easy communication, by railway, steamer, and telegraph, we are apt to think of our forefathers, without these advantages, as almost necessarily chained to their homes; and imagine the difficulties of travelling so great for them, that we infer that they did not travel at all. But this is, I think, a great mistake. The campaigns of Marlborough alone[6] must have taken a multitude of our countrymen abroad, and no doubt the bric-a-brac dealer of the period would follow at a safe distance, to pick up what he could in the track of the

armies. Paris, Florence, and Rome, have *always* been a source of attraction to architects, men of letters, men of leisure; and when men
travelled less often and more deliberately, beyond doubt they travelled to more purpose. The intercourse between our Stuart kings and
the French court was close and intimate; and we constantly find in
history accounts of men of wealth and influence bringing highly
skilled workmen to England, from Flanders, from Italy, and from
France, to produce articles of luxury of which our manufacturers
were ignorant. Moreover, there was an infinitely stronger bond of
social intercourse between the French and English[7] peoples than ever
has existed since the Revolution. And last, but not least, a craze,
which lasted a long time, and has not even yet quite departed, in
favour of France and French taste, had set in with extraordinary
ardour during the reigns of our first two Georges (George I., 1714.-1727;
George II., 1727-1760).

The attention of men like Chippendale being thus turned to French
taste, let us see what means would be readily within their reach for
obtaining the Louis Quatorze style in all its details.

Jacques Androuet, called "du Cerceau," a Frenchman, had published a book in 1550 (twice afterwards reprinted), which, besides a
good deal purely Pompeian in design, contained quite enough of what
we now call "Louis Quatorze" to instruct a man with Chippendale's
adaptability. The leg of a table or a chair, ending in an eagle's or dog's
claw, and ornamented at the top with a low relief acanthus leaf, is
there exactly; and what Chippendale calls his "terms" (bases for busts,
&c.) seem to have been copied straight off from Androuet. The carver's foliage for mirrors in Androuet's second book is so exactly what
Chippendale produced that one feels he must have had a copy of this
charming little book, just such as a carver would buy. If you add to
all this the curved "cabriole" leg, a form of terminal, whether of chair,
table, or cabinet, which at once distinguishes the feeling of the design
from its architectural predecessors, you have a distinctive character-

istic of our "Chippendale" furniture. I have not found any illustrated book, so early as Androuet's, with this form distinctly given, but historical pieces of furniture of German or Flemish work, as early as 1620, are in existence, showing it in full development; and it is more than probable that some such pieces of furniture would find their way to London during Marlborough's campaigns.

A French cabinetmaker, Jean le Pautre, published several books, illustrating chimney-pieces and overmantels,—extravagant truly, but scarcely more so than some of Chippendale's designs. His principal work is entitled *Oeuvres d'Architecture*, &c. (3 vols. folio, Paris, 1751).

These books, together, would be sufficient to instruct *all* our cabinetmakers in the details of the French Renaissance. They are full of power, but altogether deficient in restraint—the very weakness of Chippendale himself.

An important book by Charles le Brun (Paris, 1672, *et seq.*) was not likely to have been overlooked by such men as Adam and Darly, and was in all respects useful, both for the architect and the cabinetmaker. A still more important book, wider in its range of subject, by J. Berain (Paris, 1663, *et seq.*)—and another, where Berain worked in company with Chauveau and Le Moine, 1710, were sure to be known to men who could write in French on furniture and decoration; and here are the models for Chippendale's fluttering ribands for chairbacks.

D. Marot (Amsterdam, 1712) published a beautiful book of design, in which one at once sees the source of Chippendale's tall clockcases. The English productions are plainer, but all the leading lines figure in this book.

G. C. Erassmus (Nurnberg, 1659, *et seq.*) gives the exact prototype of the highly ornamental mirror-frame of Lock, Johnson, and Chippendale, and plates of "swags" of flowers, and other ornaments, all in full light and shade: a treasure-house for a carver and gilder, when such books were scarce.

A book by Boucher, Ranson, and Lalonde (Paris, undated), would give Chippendale patterns of extravagant beds and sofas to his heart's content.

And though it is somewhat difficult to determine whether the furniture part of *Dictionnaire des Sciences, des Arts et des Métiers*, small folio (Paris, no date), was published before or after Chippendale's book, yet here is his vulgar rococo sofa; and if he did not copy it from that book, both were copied from a common source of a little earlier date.

Grinling Gibbons, who died in 1721, and left many pupils behind him, would do much to make some advances towards causing French taste to be more easily appreciated; and between 1641 and 1737 several French cabinetmakers, less known to fame[8], published illustrated books of furniture. And still more to the point, *mirrors*, with highly ornamental frames, began to be a much-admired and coveted article in France in 1650; and so greatly was the importance of this article esteemed as a decoration for the houses of the rich, that the Duke of Buckingham brought glassworkers from Venice, in order to establish this manufacture, and settled them at Lambeth—a trade which still lingers there.

Now the Chippendales, father and son, were, as I have said, principally carvers; and carving of high merit was manifestly a characteristic of English decorative art of the period. Copeland, who, in point of time, seems the first of the publishers of these illustrations, was also a carver. Chippendale, to be sure, became a maker of all sorts of furniture, but a large proportion of the men whose illustrated books we possess, dated 1746 and onwards, were *carvers only*[9]; and I cannot help thinking, that the demand for ornamentally framed mirrors (a most attractive novelty to those who could pay for them, and had fine reception rooms) was largely the origin of the whole movement, so far as the cabinetmakers were concerned. The glass mirror itself had had a comparatively late origin in Venice; from Italy it had passed to

France; and it was inevitable that an Englishman should receive it framed in Renaissance taste, and that the Renaissance of France.

It is somewhat difficult to see *what was the aim* of these architects, cabinetmakers, and decorators. Did they not know that the "Renaissance" of classical form and feeling had been going on, for at least three centuries, in Italy, in Belgium, in France? Had they only just awakened to the fact? Or, did they contemplate the creation of a little renaissance for themselves? That this latter must have been the idea of such men as Adam and Richardson is evident; but it is most comical to consider the mental condition of Chippendale, Sheraton, and other cabinetmakers, posing before their beloved five orders as "the very soul and basis of art," "the true and only fount of real art," &c., and calling all men to assist them in a return to those forms and principles; and then accepting, with avidity, the most ultra-French development of a Renaissance now grown old, and not a little the worse for wear!

One cannot but see that, for them at least, the whole pretended desire for a neo-classicism was a mere pandering to the dilettanteism of the day; that they felt that to appear as high-class designers, it was desirable to follow as closely as possible in the footsteps of Wren, Inigo Jones, and the rest; and then, having appeased their consciences by an extravagant preface, and opening chapters, about the "fount of pure art," &c., they could, with a better grace, give illustrations of *what would sell*; that being, in the main, French Renaissance; no matter that it was as far in spirit from "the only fount" as Gothic itself.

But French Renaissance was a style eminently well calculated, in furniture at least, to meet the wants of well-to-do people; and the banks of prejudice having once been broken down, the flood came, and swept the devoted five orders into the sea.

It was impossible that Chippendale and Darly's style—applied, as it was, to every furniture requirement in a well-to-do house—should have sprung into existence in a decade, or even in two; for no good art work ever grew up of a sudden, like a mushroom, but always has been a development of a previous success. Still, it is interesting to note the evidences which Chippendale himself affords us of an earlier parentage of the style. First, he gives us—an early plate of the first edition (1754)—two chairs, with perspective lines about them: one of them perfectly plain, such as one sees in an old farmhouse; and again a plate of six chair-backs, also relatively plain and severe. These two plates are in contrast to the rest of the book, and he passes them by as of no moment, as if to suggest, "These are the ordinary things of ordinary people; my mission is to make grander things for the nobility and gentry!" Then, also early in his first edition, he gives the same chair over-loaded with ornament to a degree which, to our eyes, ruins it; and one cannot escape the conviction that he found the chair in the plainer condition, and that the ornamentation was his part of the business. The chair, of course, must have been invented plain, and the ornament must have come afterwards.

So that I think we cannot assign a later date for the infancy of the style than about the beginning of the eighteenth century. Many circumstances seem to have conspired about this time to produce a great start forward in adapting all the surroundings of the well-to-do to a vastly improved condition of material comfort and dignity of life; while, at the same time, the class so environed was increasing rapidly in numbers. English society was awakening from a past of comparative rudeness and barbarism; the burgher, merchant, and yeoman were now beginning to enjoy a share of the position, distinction, and wealth, hitherto the monopoly of the soldier, the aristocrat, and the courtier; the arts of peace were beginning to be respected and admired; and, simultaneously with the energy of the movement, or perhaps actually proceeding from it, there rose, as it were, a fine wave of vigorous designing power with a corresponding power of practical application.

Chippendale was in a position to feel these new conditions quickly (having, through his father, I imagine, already a connection among wealthy people, for highly ornamental mirrors and the like), and was able to take the tide "at the flood"; so that, notwithstanding his constant tendency to foolish and vulgar ornamentation, there is some justice in our having called the style by his name.

It is greatly to be regretted, however, that, instead of giving us plates, nine-tenths of which are mere "show-pieces," intended to tempt wealthy people, he did not give a volume of drawings of the average daily produce of his workshop. For nowhere, throughout his book, do we find drawings of the very best furniture then made: to almost every design he adds a coating of over-ornamentation, now Flamboyant—now Gothic—now "Chinese!" and to see the cream of the productions of his period, one has to go to the well-appointed house of a rich man—to the occasional auctions—or, to the bric-a-brac shop.[10]

Nevertheless, his plates, in the aggregate, with useless ornament omitted (he frequently calls attention to the possibility of this), do give us the main elements of the style, and are consequently valuable. Heppelwhite and Sheraton were both more practical, and so, in a sense, their designs are individually of more interest. But, as we approach Sheraton's time, the vigour and originality of the movement were fast beginning to disappear; and with a rapidity which is quite remarkable, all that was potent and virile in it completely vanished; so that it is difficult to find a design dated 1800 and onwards which is worth attention. The wave that had transformed our home surroundings had ebbed, and left us stranded; stranded, too, in the times of the fourth George and his successor—a period devoid of interest or of power—flat, stale, and unprofitable—from which we have but lately emerged.

Let me enumerate some of the leading men who contributed to the movement, and, as far as the dates of their books go, in chronological order.

W. JONES

(4to, London, 1739)

He apparently has the honour of being about the first of those who have left us an illustrated book bearing upon our subject. He calls himself an architect, and gives many illustrations of a sort of neo-classicism (far better done, a little later, by the brothers Adam). His mirrors and chimney-pieces, however, have merit, and his book is modest and unassuming.

INIGO JONES AND KENT

(Folio, London, 1744.)

Some of Inigo Jones's chimney-pieces are good, though ponderous. There is the air of the competent architect about them, as one might expect, and for halls of large houses or public buildings they might well be useful. How he came to ally himself with Kent it is not easy to understand, Kent's part of the work being weak and worthless.

H. COPELAND

(1746)

Plates are occasionally obtainable, signed H. Copeland, and dated 1746. They may have been his first attempts in this direction, and never put together in book-form. They consist of mirror-frames only, and point, as mentioned elsewhere, to the mirror as having possibly originated the illustrated furniture books.

THOMAS CHIPPENDALE

(First Edition, folio, London, 1754; Second Edition,

folio, 1759; Third Edition, folio, 1762.)

It is rather disconcerting to find this man, to whom, in common parlance, we agree to attribute our style (and who certainly has left us an abundance of copperplate engravings), not only not a man of education and modesty, but a very commonplace and vulgar hawker of his wares, prepared to make *anything* that will please his customers and fill his purse.

He calls his book "The Gentleman and Cabinetmaker's Director," "being a large collection of the most elegant and useful designs of household furniture, in the Gothic, Chinese, and modern taste". "To which is prefixed a short explanation of the five orders of architecture, and rules of perspective, with proper directions for executing the most difficult pieces," &c. "Calculated to improve and refine the present taste," &c.; then follows a quotation from Ovid, and another from Horace. He dedicates it to the Earl of Northumberland, in the usual inflated style of the period: "My lord, your intimate acquaintance with all those arts and sciences that tend to perfect and adorn life," &c. Then, under a very pretty headpiece (probably Italian), he commences his preface in this bombastic style "Of all the arts which are either improved or ornamented by architecture, that of cabinetmaking is the most useful and ornamental." (He does not see that at this precise time English cabinetmakers had begun to desert architectural lines and guidance.) "I have therefore prefixed to the following designs a short explanation of the five orders. Without an acquaintance with this science, and some knowledge of the rules of perspective, the cabinetmaker cannot make the rules of his work intelligible: ... they are the very soul and basis of his art." (It is worthy of remark that his perspective generally spoils his drawings of chairs, where the back legs seem misplaced and ridiculous, and elsewhere it always seems pedantic and out of place.) Then he talks about "the Venus of Apelles, and the Jove of Phidias". He expects adverse criticism, but says, "I shall repay their censures with contempt—they have neither good nature to commend, judgment to correct, nor skill to execute what they find fault with." He appears to have been conscious that many of his designs could hardly be put into practical shape (an accusation which Sheraton, in 1791, does not hesitate to make in the plainest terms), for he says, "I will not scruple to attribute this to malice, ignorance, and inability; and I am confident I can convince all noblemen, gentlemen, and others who will honour me with their commands," &c. Granting that this smacks mainly of the false literary style of the eighteenth century, let us see what indications we can find of his personal taste and discrimination. He says, "Plate XVI. is three riband back chairs, which . . . are the best I have ever seen (or perhaps have ever been made)," &c. But the riband is almost the worst type of ornament which the Chippendale chair ever carried. "Plates XXI. and XXII. are six new designs of Gothic (!) chairs; and Plates XXIII., XXIV., and XXV. are nine chairs in the present Chinese manner (!), which I hope will improve that taste. . . . I think it *the most useful* of any other" (the italics are mine). We talk of the "Chippendale style" nowadays, as if Chippendale had been mainly the inventor, certainly the chief expositor of it, yet here he is giving equal prominence to Gothic (the very worst of what we now recognise as "Churchwarden's Gothic"), and greater prominence still to would-be "Chinese"! "Plate XXXI. is a domed bed; . . . there are four dragons going up from each corner. The head-board has a small temple with a joss or Chinese god; on each side is a Chinese man at worship," &c. His designs for beds are miracles of false and foolish taste, and one cannot believe that he ever anticipated that the bulk of them would be carried into execution. Further on he refers to a "Gothic" bookcase as "one of the best of its kind, and would give me great pleasure to see it executed, as I doubt not of its making an exceeding genteel and grand appearance;" while the next plate but one "is a desk and bookcase in the Chinese taste, and will look extremely well." He is evidently delighted with his "Chinese" designs—"nine designs of chairs after the Chinese manner . . . they will suit Chinese temples".

After reading a few pages written in this style, one stares in amazement at his glorification of the five orders, and the pedantically exact drawings of each of them in careful detail (probably done for him by his friend and helper, Matthew Darly, an architect—see further on). Was this, and the magniloquent talk about perspective, genuine? or was it merely intended to give his book an architectural and scientific air? One cannot resist the suspicion, for he never seemed to try for a moment to bring his five orders into practical use for his cabinets. We can afford to smile now at this cabinetmaker vapouring about his neo-Greek, but no doubt it was then thought by the "noblemen, gentlemen, and others" to whom he addressed himself, that all good art must flow from Greece as a fountain-head, and it would sound and look well to begin directly from Greek temples. Nevertheless, the eager tradesman could not but peep out, and in spite of "the true fount of art," he found that "Gothic" and "Chinese" chairs and cabinets would *sell*, and he puffed them accordingly, and that rather more than his French Renaissance designs. To work even as near the neo-Greek as the Adams, he makes not the feeblest attempt.

His most ambitious designs are, I imagine, merely advertising suggestions of what he is prepared to make, if he can get orders— witness Plate CXI., "a China case, not only the richest and most magnificent in the whole, but perhaps in all Europe. . . . I should have much pleasure in the execution of it," &c.

There is a plate alluded to above (No. XVI. in the third edition), consisting of six backs of chairs—simple and severe, quite the best of his chair designs, and appearing to belong to the early stage of the developments of the "Chip" chair, though not in the first edition. He passes this plate by without a word of comment, although almost every other plate has a few words, and often several sentences of praise.

So that, with every desire to accord the utmost value to Chippendale's book, and valuable it certainly is, as the earliest and most comprehensive exponent of the style, one cannot for a moment rank its author as a man of "taste." His desire to pander to any sort of trumpery fancy of the hour, now so-called "Chinese," now extravagant Louis Quatorze, now "Churchwarden's Gothic," led him into continual trouble; for, going carefully through the third edition (which does not differ materially from the first), and, with every desire to be fair and broadminded, dividing the designs into four groups, one comes to some such result as this—Good, 60; Passable (i.e., designs with merit in them, but partially spoiled by false detail), 103; Fantastic and foolish, 146; with a remainder of 107 which can only be called preposterous, impossible, or outrageous. That is to say, the good and passable are scarcely as two to three of the others.

Later, he published a 4to book of designs (undated) for "Sconces, Chimney and Looking-glass frames in the old French style" (the only place in which I can find any acknowledgment of his indebtedness to the French), which is at once commonplace, vulgar, and largely impracticable.

EDWARDS AND DARLEY

(4to, London, 1754. Darley, spelt also Darly.)

"A new book of Chinese designs," &c. The Chinese mania appears to have been raging rather fiercely just then, probably owing to the significant influence of Sir William Chambers, who, however, did not appear in print until rather later. There are some drawings of flowers and birds in this book, in the Chinese manner, worth passing attention, but otherwise it is a mere tissue of folly and weakness.

THOMAS JOHNSON

(Small folio, Westminster, 1758, and small 4to, London, 1761.)

Johnson was a carver, and his book mainly consists of designs for girandoles, picture-frames, mirror-frames, and candlesticks-no chairs, tables, or cabinets. Curiously, this book is dedicated, on a florid and pedantic title-page, to Lord Blakeney, "*Grand President of the Anti-Gallican Association,*" the designs being, however, extremely French. Probably he feels that he may defend himself somewhat by adding, "It is a duty incumbent on an author to endeavour at pleasing every taste!" His designs are quite as foolish and impossible as the worst of Chippendale's, though not quite so pretentious. In 1761 he published a smaller *réchauffé* of the book, very stupid and vulgar; some of the girandoles are incredibly false and foolish.

INCE AND MAYHEW

(Folio, London, undated, but probably earlier than 1760.)

The title-page, both English and French, describes the book to be "in the most elegant taste"; "the whole made convenient to the nobility and gentry." There is a flowery inscription to the Duke of Marlborough; and we are informed—"and with same regard any gentleman may furnish as neat at a small expense as he can elegant and superb at a great one" (*sic*). Matthias Darly, the assistant of Chippendale, appears to have been engaged as engraver, and the book purports to be partly "a drawing-book adapted to young beginners," who are to copy excessively rococo and florid ornament, like the most extreme French work. They give plates of excessively over-ornamented "Chip" chairs, and beds quite as absurd and vulgar as Chippendale's —indeed, all these men seemed to lose their heads the moment they designed a bed. Some of the dressing-tables and chests of drawers are fairly good, though none seem quite worth reproducing. There is the absurd disposition to be "Chinese" which we have seen in others of this period, and "un grand sofa" rather out-chippendales Chippendale in its gross vulgarity. Altogether it might be described as a foolish and worthless book, unworthy of notice, were it not for its important size, costly plates, and presumably early date.

A SOCIETY OF UPHOLSTERERS

(4to, London, no date, which I presume to be about 1760.
Entitled "Genteel Household Furniture.")

There is no preface, and the names of designers and engravers are mostly omitted. The plates consist largely of chairs—Gothic chairs, Chinese chairs, and very florid "Chip" chairs, these last being a sort of false and clumsy travesty of Louis Quatorze work. But suddenly, in the middle of the book comes a plate of altogether different style —no designer's name given, but inscribed "Couse sculpt."—a cabinet, not important, but severe, simple, and pretty. It is repeated, with slight alterations, several times, and like Chippendale's six chair-backs, alluded to above, seems to point back to an earlier and purer condition of the style. The compilers give an illustration of a nice wrought-iron balcony, two or three bits of pretty iron-work for the brackets of inn signboards, such as one still sees in Barnet and else-where, and a good ornamental chain for a candelabrum; but other-wise the book is devoid of interest, and may be considered a copy of Chippendale, and not of Chippendale's best. They also published a second edition, and two appendices, of no special value.

MATTHIAS LOCK

(4to, London, 1765-68; also post 4to, no date; also oblong 4to, 1769.)

Lock was a carver, and his works are mainly interesting as helping to show that this series of books on furniture, rapidly following each other, was originated, as elsewhere observed, by the carvers. Lock is ultra-French and fantastic in his designs, and, in his higher flights, often very vulgar. His books may be considered useless. The South Kensington Museum contains a folio of original sketches, with a few prints from steel or copper plates interspersed, ascribed to Lock and H. Copeland (mentioned above), and containing, amid numerous scrappy details of the carver, some lovely drawings of a plant of the acanthus tribe, presumably for carving from. The chairs are not good, and there is nothing else worthy of notice.

ROBERT MANWARING AND OTHERS

(8vo, London, 1766. "The Chairmaker's Guide; 200 New and Genteel Designs.")

Manwaring was evidently the moving spirit of the "Society of Upholsterers" mentioned above; for they published a second edition, undated, to many of the designs in which Manwaring now added his name; and the book, published in 1766, where his name appears on the title-page, contains a great many of the very plates previously used for the Society's book. He gives a large number of illustrations of "Chip" chairs, but never manages to draw a really good one. The "Gothic" chairs are rather worse than one had thought possible. The "Hall" chairs are quite preposterous.

N. WALLIS, ARCHITECT

(Oblong 4to, London, 1771. Entitled "A Book of Ornaments."

Also, oblong 4to, 1772, "The Complete Modern Joiner.")

Wallis has a simple and modest title-page and preface; and though he is beset by the fear of departing by one jot or tittle from his supposed Greek models, yet his book is well worth examination, being free from rubbish, and full of most excellent chimney-pieces.

R. AND J. ADAM

(First Edition, 3 vols. folio, London, 1773, et seq.)

Their book is entitled "The Works in Architecture of Robert and James Adam, Esquires," and is printed in parallel columns of French and English, in large folio, on splendid paper, *édition de luxe*. Robert appears to have been mainly the designer. The work was published in numbers and parts, and was continued from 1773 to 1779. After their death in 1822, a further part was published, but it is of quite inferior interest.

This noble work, splendid alike in design, in draughtsmanship, in execution, and in taste, must surely have had a share in forming the national style, probably greater than all the other books we are considering put together. For though it is called an architectural work, and is entirely passed in silence by Sheraton when he discusses his competitors' works, it contains far more plates of articles of furniture than many of the so-called furniture books; and besides thirty-two designs for chimney-pieces, ceilings, cornices, &c., which may rightly be considered as entirely architectural, it gives us no less than sixty-four designs for mirrors, sconces, draped cornices, side-tables, bookcases, clocks, lamps, &c., all well worth reproducing. For the brothers Adam justly considered all the fittings of a house as coming within the scope of their art; and if we could only be sure that our architects possessed the Adams' taste and discretion, nothing could be more desirable than that they should undertake them now.

To be sure, they were religiously devoted to those worshipful five orders, and they tied themselves, as tightly as ever they knew how, to that arbitrary standard; and, in consequence, their designs are often wanting in freedom, and at times in adaptability to the end in view; and one cannot help continually stopping to wonder, if they could do so much, restrained by such inelastic leading strings, what might they not have done if their sympathies had had a wider base? But we must take the past as we find it; and, considering the vile taste which surrounded them on all sides—the false standards set up by a pretended admiration of classic work on the one hand, and an extravagant desire to follow all the excesses of the French Renaissance on the other — we cannot be too thankful for this splendid work.

The frontispiece and preface, one must confess, are not a little trying. "A student conducted to Minerva, who points to Greece and Italy as the countries from whence he must derive the most perfect knowledge of taste," &c., forms the title of a large and ultra-showy frontispiece; and in the preface they claim to have themselves "in some measure brought about a kind of revolution in the whole system of this beautiful and elegant art" (architecture), "and in the decoration of the inside, an almost total change." "It seems to have been reserved for the present time to see compartment ceilings carried to a degree of perfection in Great Britain that far surpasses any of the former attempts of other modern nations." "Whether our works have not contributed to diffuse these improvements through this country, we shall leave to the impartial public; . . . we flatter ourselves we have been able to seize, with some degree of success, the beautiful spirit of antiquity, and to transfuse it with novelty and variety through all our numerous works!" They go on to claim that they have designed "every kind of ornamental furniture." "The style of the ornament and the colouring of the Countess of Derby's dressing-room (imitated from vases of the Etruscans) show the first idea of applying this taste to the decoration of apartments!" "In architecture, Inigo Jones rescued us from Gothicism; Wren was enabled to exhibit his genius in St. Paul's; Vanbrugh understood the art of living among the great;" and the brothers Adam "claim to have carried on and completed the diffusion of better taste!" Clearly, they were not free from the charge of false taste in preface-writing, but we must allow a good deal for the bombastic literary style of the period, and we forgive the high-sounding talk, when we open the book. Its weakness, for the purposes of this inquiry, is that the Adams seem to have designed entirely for rich people, who, one would think, never considered the cost of anything; and this to some extent lands the work among specialities and museum collections, and deprives it of that all-round adaptability, which must be the characteristic of a really vital style, which is to become traditional. Still, a large proportion of their ornament is capable of being executed cheaply in carton-pierre and plaster, and often forms the chaste and delicate ornamental touch of many a burgher's house, of somewhat later date. If our speculating builders would only take their plaster cornices, to go no further, from this admirable book, what a stride would be made at once towards the better decoration of our rooms! And architects and decorators of public buildings might here find a quarry from' which they might dig nearly all their material, greatly to the advantage of the whole nation.

MATTHIAS DARLY

(Small folio, London, 1773. Entitled "A Compleat Body of Architecture, embellished with
a great variety of ornaments," compiled, drawn, and engraved by Matthias Darly,
Professor of Ornament.)

Darly, I think, must have been brought up as an architect, but preferred the ornamental side of his art. He says—"Ornamental drawing" (drawing of ornament) "has been too long neglected in this trading country, and great losses have been sustained in many of our manufactures for want of it. On the knowledge of true embellishment depends the improvement of every article, and I do aver that this kingdom is more indebted to a Richd. Langcake (who is now teaching the art of design in France[11]) than to a Sir Godfrey Kneller." He claims his book to be "the first and only publication of the kind"(!). "Many authors" (on architecture) "content themselves with giving only the proportion, and almost totally neglect the graceful addition of ornament; to supply which defect this work is principally intended."

Besides matters more strictly architectural, he gives plates of ceilings, panels, chimney-pieces, vases, spandrils, brackets, frames, friezes, &c. He appears to have worked for Chippendale, both as a designer and as an engraver. His "frames" and "panels" are frequently most elegant and graceful pieces of composition, far in advance of his contemporaries, if we except Adam and Pergolesi. In ceiling designs he seems to be the equal of Robert Adam. If he sins, it is by omission. He never attempts a table, chair, or cabinet. But his designs have, almost without exception, some merit, and are never foolish or pretentious. In 1767, before his principal work, he published a book, oblong 4to, entitled "Sixty Vases by English, French, and Italian Masters"—one of the very few hints that we get that these men knew, or were willing to admit, that they were borrowing from the French.

The following may be bracketed as inferior productions of no merit, and quite useless: A. Rosis, small folio, 1753, "New Book of Ornament; "Manwaring, London, 1765, "The Carpenter's Complete Guide;" "The Cabinet and Chairmaker's Real Friend and Companion," by the same, also 1765; "The Carpenter's Companion for Chinese Railings and Gates" (H. Morris and J. Crunden, 1770); and "The Joyner and Cabinetmaker's Darling" (John Crunden, 1770); Gaetano Brunetti, "Sixty Different Sorts of Ornament," 4to, 1736; J. Gibbs, 4to, 1731, "Thirty-three Shields and Compartments," &c.; Wm. Halfpenny, 8vo, 1750, "New Designs for Chinese Temples, &c.,"

P. COLUMBANI

(4to, London, 1775, "A New Book of Ornaments." Also
4to, 1776, "A Variety of Capitals.")

Two modest and business-like performances, containing panel ornament and excellent chimney-pieces, almost equal to the designs of Adam and Richardson. The scope and extent of the books, however, hardly entitle them to an important place.

GEORGE RICHARDSON

(Folio, 1776. Entitled "A Book of Ceilings." Also
folio, 1781, "A New Collection of Chimney-pieces.")

Richardson was a gentleman and a scholar. After disclaiming with a charming honesty any real classic authority for his designs (which are very much on the lines of Robert Adam), he says—"The following designs are composed in the style of the present improved taste." This nice feeling pervades the book; and as he is certainly less in awe of the five orders than his predecessors, and gives more variety of style and ornament than the others (though always strictly within limited boundaries, it is not too much to say that he is *facile princeps* in chimney-piece drawing. There is not a foolish or impracticable design in the book, and most of them address themselves to a middle-class public rather than to the millionaire. He published several other books, mostly more strictly architectural, and one, consisting of ceilings only (folio, 1776), on thick paper, got up very much after the style of the Adams' book, inevitably suggesting a sense of rivalry with that splendid work, published three years previously. It is free from ostentation or vulgarity, but is deficient in freedom, as if he were chained fast again to the inevitable "orders."

There were several other architects who assisted in the movement, such as James Gibbs, "A Book of Architecture," fol. 1739; Abm. Swan, "A Collection of Designs in Architecture," fol. 1757; Swan again, "The British Architect," fol. 1758; Swan again, "Designs in Carpentry," 4to, 1759; W. Thomas, "Original Designs in Architecture," fol. 1783; W. and J. Pain, fol. 1786, "Pains' British Palladio;" the Pains again, fol. 1793; B. and T. Longley, "The Builder's Jewel," 16mo, 1787; R. Morris, royal 8vo, "The Architect's Remembrancer;" J. Wyatt, "Original Coloured Drawings of Ornaments to Scale," no date, about 1770; Thos. Milton, John Crunden, Placido Columbani (mentioned above), and T. C. Overton, four, working together, and producing "The Chimney-Piece-Maker's

Daily Assistant," imp. 8vo, 1766; but I pass them by on account of the very inferior interest of their productions when weighed against Adam, Richardson, Darly, and Pergolesi. The first four have been well reproduced by R. Charles, "The Compiler," London, 1879

M. A. PERGOLESI

(Folio, London, 1777, *et seq.*)

A valuable and charming book of ornament, without preface, and merely entitled, "Designs." It is somewhat restricted in its scope, and follows, like the Adams' work, a too severe adhesion to the supposed hard and fast limits imposed by those tyrannous "five orders." Nevertheless he breaks away inevitably, (further perhaps than he knew,) from his jailors, and leaves us a very interesting and useful book, which forms a good hunting ground for designers today, though not old enough to belong to the great days of art.

It appears to have been published in numbers extending over some years, and existing copies are seldom complete. In the later numbers there are "centres" to panelled ornaments, engraved by Bartolozzi (amorini, and the like), which are most lovely. Indeed, to lovers of ornament, it is a delightful book, and perfect copies are worth probably ten times the original cost. Pergolesi was brought from Italy by Robert Adam, and, beyond doubt, was the unacknowledged author of most of the beautiful details of the Adams' book.

G. B. CIPRIANI

(Folio, London, 1786.)

A book of ornament—figure-work only—engraved by Bartolozzi, and not important to the present inquiry, is the only one of Cipriani's books published in England, in 1786—the rest (for he published several date from Rome, and are much later. Nevertheless, he cannot be overlooked as a factor in the movement, for, like Angelica Kauffmann, he constantly provided elegant little designs for the panels and backs of Sheraton and Heppelwhite's sofas and chairs, and what he did in this way he did well.

THE CABINETMAKER'S LONDON
BOOK OF PRICES
(Small 4to, London, 1788. Second Edition, 1793.)

The best designs are signed "Shearer." Shearer is excellent and practical, never ostentatious or pretentious. He certainly does not rise to the highest flights possible to the style, but he is always sound and moderate, and never descends to showy rubbish. One wishes that his 29 plates had been 92.

A. HEPPELWHITE & CO.
(Foolscap folio, London, 1789. "The Cabinetmaker and Upholsterer's Guide.")

The authors commence in the stilted style of the time—"To unite elegance with utility, and blend the useful with the agreeable, has ever been considered a difficult but an honourable task." It is "in the newest and most approved taste." "English taste and workmanship have, of late years, been much sought for by surrounding nations" (?) . . . "and the mutability of all things, but more especially of fashion, has rendered the labours of our predecessors in this line of little use!" Their book is "useful to the mechanic, serviceable to the gentleman," and "we designedly followed the latest fashion only." This last statement is certainly true enough, in the sense that the style, since Chippendale's time, had already made a considerable development, partly in the direction of Louis Quinze work—chairs with their straight-fluted and beaded legs, for instance—and partly in the direction of an English sobriety of taste, alluded to above.

But beyond this high-sounding preface, Heppelwhite appears merely as the plain unvarnished tradesman with an illustrated list of wares to sell; and a very practical and excellent list it is. We can see his tea-caddies, tea-trays, tops of card-tables and dressing-tables, are most charming examples of beautiful design and arrangement. He seems to have benefited considerably by the labours of Pergolesi: his beds are, as usual, too ambitious, and he loses his head somewhat about draped cornices; but the book, taken as a whole, is quite useful and modest, and nearly always quite practicable, so that among his 300 designs there are scarcely twenty which might not, with advantage, be reproduced.

THOMAS SHERATON

(4to, London, 1791-93. Entitled "The Cabinet Maker and Upholsterer's Drawing Book."
An "appendix" to the above, 4to, 1793; "an accompaniment," 4to, 1794.; a "Cabinet
Dictionary," 8vo, 1803; "Designs for Household Furniture," folio, 1804; "The Cabinet
Maker, Upholsterer, and General Artist's Encyclopedia. Coloured Plates," folio, 1804.)

Sheraton, though more modest than Chippendale, cannot commence his book without recourse to those never-to-be-forgotten five orders, and "geometrical instructions for finding lines for Hip and Elliptic domes for State beds". Part II. he titles "on practical perspective . . . together with a little of the theory for such as would know some of the reasons on which their useful art is founded." And he cannot resist a frontispiece, representing "Geometry standing on a rock with Perspective by his side," &c., "while on the background is the Temple of Fame, to which a knowledge of these arts directly leads". He says it will not be "requisite to use an ostentatious preface," and immediately proceeds to write one.

He gives a little account of his predecessors "I have seen (a book) which seems to have been published before Chippendale"—he mentions no date—"but it is of no value, because it gives no instructions in drawing". "Chippendale's book seems to be next in order to this, but the designs themselves are now wholly antiquated and laid aside" (Chip., third edition, 1762; Sheraton, 1791-93). He mentions Manwaring's book (1766), and says—"There is nothing in his directions but what an apprentice boy may be taught in seven hours . . . the geometrical views of the five orders are useful, and the only thing in his book which at this day is worth notice, as his chairs are nearly all as old as Chippendale's, and seem to be copied from them." Of Ince and Mayhew's book he says—"The designs are of such kind as are wholly laid aside in the cabinet branch."

Of Heppelwhite's book, published in 1789, he says—"Some of these designs are not without merit, but if we compare the chairs with the newest date, we shall find that this work has already caught the decline" (i.e., in two years!). He thinks his own book "will be found greatly to supply the defects of those now mentioned" (he entirely ignores R. and J. Adam), for "it is pretty evident that the materials for proper ornament are now brought to such perfection as will not in future admit of much, if any, improvement". He occupies 311 pages out of 446 in his first book with elaborate instructions as to geometrical, architectural, and perspective drawing—some of which might possibly be useful to an architect who had a town-hall to design, but are totally useless and cumbersome for cabinetmakers, to whom alone he addresses himself; and one cannot avoid the suspicion that he felt jealous of the brothers Adam, and wished to show that he could do their own work better.

He could occasionally be preposterous, as some elaborate plates of beds witness; but he is, in general, far more reasonable, severe, and practical than Chippendale, though it must be admitted that he does not cover so much ground. I think there can be little doubt that he had had some architectural education, and had drifted into cabinetmaking. There is a plate introduced after No. LV. which differs considerably from all the others in the book (though marked as Sheraton's drawing, and engraved by the same hand as the rest), which must have been inspired by a sense of rivalry with Robert Adam; and, in a most pedantic way, he goes at length into a question, whether or no Solomon's temple was Doric architecture!—or possibly Tuscan! —arguing the matter with dates, dimensions, proportions, &c.—in fact, he is (or pretends to be) wrapped up in his beloved five orders, and the transition from Greek temples to chair backs is as amusing as it is sudden.

There is good wheat, beyond doubt, in the "appendix," and the "accompaniment," although there is an immense proportion of chaff; but his books do not improve as the series goes on, and the last, the "Encyclopaedia," in which the "Designs for Household Furniture" were included, is pretentious and rambling in scope, and the illustrations, in the fashion of the day (1804), coloured, are incredibly false and vulgar, exhibiting a deterioration, in the eleven years from his first book, which is quite remarkable.

In the three earlier books, however (and it is through these that his memory will survive), notwithstanding all his bombast in the letterpress, he is never so pretentious as Chippendale, and his proportion of good work is considerably greater. Intellectually, he seems to have been a man nearer the calibre of the Adams, and he had evidently caught the improvement in severity of line which was taking place in good French work (Louis Quinze, 1715-1774), and had added a sobriety to it which he had not caught from France. The best of his chairs are still in high repute, and they have probably fetched higher prices (relative to their importance and cost) than any of the furniture we are discussing.

But here we come, rather suddenly, to an end of the men whose works are of value. J. Taylor, about 1805, published a book entitled "Decorative Household Furniture"; but the entire absence of any merit whatever makes one see how completely the designing power which produced the style had passed away. G. Smith, again, in 1808, published a 4to book entitled "Collection of Designs for Household Furniture," curiously stupid and vulgar. Two or more by H. Wood, 4to, undated, probably 1806, are entirely devoid of merit; and complete impracticability had its day in 1807, when Thomas Hope published his "Household Furniture and Interior Decoration," which might have been written to show how a close and faithful adherence to Egyptian, Greek, and Roman forms is utterly incompatible with any practical attempt to meet the needs of modern home life.

I desire to acknowledge my indebtedness to Mr. J. H. Pollen's excellent book on furniture: *A Comprehensive History of Furniture-making, and its Gradual Development, From the Very Earliest Times.*

Notes

1 This, though only written a few years ago, has become a fulfilled prophecy: witness the hat-trimming of 1896.

2 This chapter was originally an address to the Liverpool Architectural Association.

3 The brothers Adam were architects, and although they designed furniture, they certainly never made any.

4 Their book is undated.

5 To be sure the Adams, Chippendale, and Sheraton all pose before us as founding themselves entirely on Greek and Roman originals, and give minute drawings and descriptions of each of the so-called "five orders". So long as they can keep to doors and windows, arcades and friezes, all is tolerably Greek and Roman; but the moment they have to design something for which they can find no Greek or Roman model, at once they descend without hesitation or apology to out-and-out French Renaissance.

6 Commenced in 1704. Peace of Utrecht, 1713. As dates are handy in such a question, here are three leading ones—Louis XIV, 1643-1715; Louis XV, 1715-1774; Louis XVI, 1744 to Revolution.

7 A curious instance of this is to be seen in a book of engravings for silversmiths, evidently for French trade with England; many of the articles depicted are entitled in English—thus, "a T pot," &c., yet the whole is manifestly French work. The South Kensington copy has no title or date, and is assigned to 1780—but looks earlier. There are 141 carefully executed steel plates, the designs being, for the most part, excellent, simple, and severe.

8 For example, J. Barbet, 1641; H. Goltzius, about 1641; P. Mignard, 1650 and 1700; Juste Aurele Meissonier, about 1670; P. Bourdon, 1703; Nicholas Pineau, 1710; Leblond, 1716; G. Brunetti, 1736; E. Bouchardon, 1737.

9 For example, Matthias Lock, 1765; Thomas Johnson, 1761; G. Lairesse, about 1750.

10 Curiously, not one of these men gives us a drawing, or even an approach to one, of the favourite little mahogany-framed mirror, carved or pierced above and below, with a gilt bird coming through a hole at the top—an ornamental object of interest to be found in half the well-furnished houses of the land, and undoubtedly an heirloom from Chippendale's time: indeed, London bric-a-brac shops have usually some on sale quite a century old, as well as copies.

11 Because he could not get employment in England.

Index

www.ingramcontent.com/pod-product-compliance
Lightning Source LLC
Chambersburg PA
CBHW031850090426
42741CB00005B/427